Witches'
Spell-A-Day
Almanac

Holidays & Lore
Spells, Rituals & Meditations

Copyright 2013 Llewellyn Worldwide Ltd.
Cover Design: Lisa Novak
Editing: Andrea Neff

Background photo: © PhotoDisc
Interior Art: © 2011, Steven McAfee
pp. 13, 33, 51, 71, 91, 111, 133, 153, 173, 195, 217, 237
Spell icons throughout: © 2011 Sherrie Thai

You can order Llewellyn books and annuals from *New Worlds*,
Llewellyn's catalog. To request a free copy of the catalog, call toll-free
1-877-NEW WRLD or visit our website at www.llewellyn.com

ISBN: 978-0-7387-2159-0
Llewellyn is a registered trademark of Llewellyn Worldwide Ltd.
2143 Wooddale Drive
Woodbury, MN 55125

Printed in the United States of America

Contents

About the Authors

Elizabeth Barrette has been involved with the Pagan community for more than 24 years. Her book *Composing Magic: How to Create Magical Spells, Rituals, Blessings, Chants, and Prayers* explains how to combine writing and spirituality. She lives in central Illinois, where she has done much networking with Pagans in her area, such as coffeehouse meetings and open sabbats; see the Greenhaven website, http://greenhaventradition.weebly .com. Her other writing fields include speculative fiction, gender studies, and social and environmental issues. Visit her blog *The Wordsmith's Forge* at http://ysabetwordsmith.livejournal.com.

Blake Octavian Blair (Carrboro, NC) is an Eclectic Pagan Witch, ordained minister, psychic, tarot reader, freelance writer, Usui Reiki Master-Teacher, musical artist, and a devotee of Lord Ganesha. He holds a degree in English and Religion from the University of Florida. In his spare time he enjoys beading jewelry and knitting and is an avid reader. Blake lives in the Piedmont region of North Carolina with his beloved husband, an aquarium full of fish, and an indoor jungle of houseplants. Visit him on the web at www.blakeoctavianblair.com or write him at blake@blakeoctavianblair.com.

Boudica is a practicing Witch and Crone who lives and works within the Pagan community as a writer, facilitator, and teacher. She works in Information Technology by day, and surfs and writes by night. She loves the Pagan community with all its diverse and colorful people. Boudica is a displaced liberal, feminist New Yorker living in the heart of the ultra-conservative Midwest. She has one husband and four cats.

Thuri Calafia is an ordained minister and Wiccan High Priestess, teacher, and founder of Circles School of Wicca and Witchcraft. She is the author of *Dedicant: A Witch's Circle of Fire* and *Initiate: A Witch's Circle of Water*, which are complete courses of study based on her teachings. She is currently working on the third book in the series, *Adept: A Witch's Circle of Earth*. She is actively involved in the Pagan community in the Pacific Northwest, and lives with her beloved partner, Robert, and their four-legged "child," Miss Alyssa Ramone.

Dallas Jennifer Cobb practices gratitude magic, giving thanks for her magical life, happy and healthy family, meaningful and flexible work, and joyous adventure. She believes that she has time, energy, wisdom, and

money to accomplish her deepest desires, and she is pursuing them all. She lives in paradise in a waterfront village in rural Ontario and chants: *Thank you, Thank you, Thank you.* Contact her at jennifer.cobb@live.com.

Kerri Connor is the High Priestess of The Gathering Grove, and has been practicing her craft for 26 years. She is the author of several books, including *Spells for Tough Times.*

Emyme, an eclectic solitary, resides in a multi-generation, multi-cat household in Southern New Jersey—concentrating on candle spells, garden spells, and kitchen witchery. In addition to writing poetry and prose about strong women of mythology and fairy tales, Emyme is creating a series of articles on bed & breakfasts from the point of view of the over-fifty-five, single, female, Wiccan traveler. Please send questions or comments to catsmeow24@verizon.net.

Michael Furie (Northern California) has been a practicing Witch for over 17 years. An American Witch, he practices in the Irish tradition and is a priest of the Cailleach. He has written articles about magic and spirituality for online Pagan websites such as witchvox.com. He enjoys cooking, reading, growing herbs, and studying herbalism, magic, and Irish lore.

James Kambos has had a lifelong interest in folk magic, and is a regular contributor to Llewellyn's annuals. He lives in Ohio, where he also paints and gardens.

Deborah Lipp is the author of six books, including *Merry Meet Again: Lessons, Life & Love on the Path of a Wiccan High Priestess* and *The Elements of Ritual: Air, Fire, Water and Earth in the Wiccan Circle.* Deborah has been Wiccan for over 30 years, and a High Priestess of the Gardnerian tradition since 1986. She's been published in *newWitch, Llewellyn's Magical Almanac, Pangaia, Green Egg,* and *The Druid's Progress.* Deborah is also an avid media writer and blogger, and is co-owner of *Basket of Kisses: Smart Discussion About Smart Television* (www.lippsisters.com). She lives in Rockland County, New York.

Mickie Mueller is an award-winning and critically acclaimed artist of fantasy, fairy, and myth. She is an ordained Pagan minister and has studied Natural Magic, Fairy Magic, and Celtic tradition. She is also a Reiki healing master/teacher in the Usui Shiki Royoho Tradition. She enjoys creating magical art full of fairies, goddesses, and beings of folklore.

Mickie is the illustrator of *The Well Worn Path* and *The Hidden Path* decks, the writer/illustrator of *Voice of the Trees: A Celtic Divination Oracle*, and the illustrator of the upcoming *Mystical Cats Tarot*, coming in 2014.

Gede Parma Akheron is a Wild Witch, Pagan Mystic, initiated Priest, and award-winning author. He is an initiate and teacher of the WildWood Tradition of Witchcraft, a hereditary healer and seer with Balinese-Celtic ancestry, and an enthusiastic writer. Gede is a proactive and dynamic teacher and is also the creator and facilitator of the two-year Shamanic Craft Apprenticeship. He teaches both within Australia and internationally. Gede's spiritual path is highly syncretic, fusing a variety of Craft and Mystic traditions. He is also the devoted priest and lover of Aphrodite, Hermes, Hekate, the Blue God, Persephone, and the Sacred Four of the WildWood.

Susan Pesznecker is a writer, college English teacher, and hearth Pagan/Druid living in northwestern Oregon. Her magickal roots include Pictish Scot and Eastern European/Native American medicine traditions. Sue holds a master's degree in nonfiction writing and loves to read, stargaze, camp with her wonder poodle, and play in her biodynamic garden. She's co-founder of the Druid Grove of Two Coasts (find the Grove on Facebook) and teaches nature studies and herbalism in the online Grey School. Sue has authored *Crafting Magick with Pen and Ink* (Llewellyn, 2009) and *The Magickal Retreat* (Llewellyn, 2012) and regularly contributes to the Llewellyn annuals. Visit her at www.susanpesznecker.com and www.facebook.com/SusanMoonwriterPesznecker.

Laurel Reufner's mother can verify that she grew up a "wild child" in farming country. Laurel has been earth-centered for nearly 25 years now and really enjoys writing about shiny topics that grab her attention. She has always lived in southeastern Ohio and currently calls Athens County home, where she lives with her wonderful husband and two wild children of her own. Find her online at oaknolive.blogspot.com.

Tess Whitehurst is the author of *The Art of Bliss, The Magic of Flowers, The Good Energy Book,* and *Magical Housekeeping.* She lives in Venice, CA. Visit her online, read her blog, and sign up for her free monthly newsletter at www.tesswhitehurst.com.

A Note on Magic and Spells

The spells in the *Witches' Spell-A-Day Almanac* evoke everyday magic designed to improve our lives and homes. You needn't be an expert on magic to follow these simple rites and spells; as you will see if you use these spells throughout the year, magic, once mastered, is easy to perform. The only advanced technique required of you is the art of visualization.

Visualization is an act of controlled imagination. If you can call up in your mind a picture of your best friend's face or a flag flapping in the breeze, you can visualize. In magic, visualizations are used to direct and control magical energies. Basically the spellcaster creates a visual image of the spell's desired goal, whether it be perfect health, a safe house, or a protected pet.

Visualization is the basis of all good spells, and as such it is a tool that should be properly used. Visualization must be real in the mind of the spellcaster so it allows him or her to raise, concentrate, and send forth energy to accomplish the spell.

Perhaps when visualizing you'll find that you're doing everything right, but you don't feel anything. This is common, for we haven't been trained to acknowledge—let alone utilize—our magical abilities. Keep practicing, however, for your spells can "take" even if you're not the most experienced natural magician.

You will notice also that many spells in this collection have a some-what "light" tone. They are seemingly fun and frivolous, filled with rhyme and colloquial speech. This is not to diminish the seriousness of the purpose, but rather to create a relaxed atmosphere for the practitio-ner. Lightness of spirit helps focus energy; rhyme and common language help the spellcaster remember the words and train the mind where it is needed. The intent of this magic is indeed very serious at times, and magic is never to be trifled with.

Even when your spells are effective, magic won't usually sparkle before your very eyes. The test of magic's success is time, not immedi-ate eye-popping results. But you can feel magic's energy for yourself by rubbing your palms together briskly for ten seconds, then holding them a few inches apart. Sense the energy passing through them, the warm tin-gle in your palms. This is the power raised and used in magic. It comes from within and is perfectly natural.

Among the features of the *Witches' Spell-A-Day Almanac* are an easy-to-use "book of days" format; new spells specifically tailored for each day of the year (and its particular magical, astrological, and historical energies); and additional tips and lore for various days throughout the year—including color correspondences based on planetary influences, obscure and forgotten holidays and festivals, and an incense of the day to help you waft magical energies from the ether into your space. Moon signs, phases, and voids are also included to help you find the perfect time for your rituals and spells.

Enjoy your days, and have a magical year!

Spells at a Glance by Date and Category*

	Health	Protection	Success	Heart, Love	Clearing, Cleaning	Home	Meditation, Divination
Jan.	14, 20, 29	5, 9, 17	1, 6, 10	24	12, 26	2, 11, 13	4, 25
Feb.	13	8, 12, 15, 27	6, 23, 25, 26		5, 9, 22	11, 16, 17, 21	
March	16, 24, 26	15, 19, 31		3, 12, 21, 22	6, 27		7, 13, 17
April		2, 7, 24, 27	6, 19	16		13	11, 23, 26
May	12, 22, 25	3, 13, 23, 28, 29	1, 30	16	26	2	5, 6, 8, 11
June		16, 19		2, 6	3, 8, 14	9, 28	
July	3, 14, 16	15, 17, 24	10, 22, 31	18, 29		27	7, 8
Aug.	22	5, 15, 18	8, 20, 31		16, 19, 29		11, 13, 23
Sept.	3, 7, 25	12, 27, 28	5, 14	15, 23		16	10, 29
Oct.	11	26		14, 18	4, 13, 20, 25	3, 6, 12	2, 7, 10, 31
Nov.	13, 18, 30	3, 19, 29	5, 23	27	14	9, 17, 20, 21, 25	2, 12, 24
Dec.	2, 12	14	27		18, 19, 23, 28	30	8, 10, 15, 24

*List is not comprehensive.

Spell–A–Day Icons

 New Moon

 Meditation, Divination

 Full Moon

 Money, Prosperity

 Abundance

 Protection

 Altar

 Relationship

 Balance

 Success

 Clearing, Cleaning

 Travel, Communication

 Garden

 Air Element

 Grab Bag

 Earth Element

 Health

 Fire Element

 Home

 Spirit Element

 Heart, Love

 Water Element

2014
Year of Spells

January

January is the first month of the year in the Gregorian calendar. On average, it is the coldest month in the Northern Hemisphere and the warmest month in the Southern Hemisphere. January is named after the Roman god Janus, the god of doorways. Janus is typically depicted with two faces, so he could see both what was behind him and what was in front of him. The side that faced the past was shown as mature and bearded, whereas the side that faced the future was youthful and full of hope. Janus's name came from the Latin word for door, *ianua*, and so January is the doorway into the new year. January is a quiet month after all the hustle and bustle of the holiday season. For those who follow the Wheel of the Year, it falls between Yule, when we celebrate the slow return of the light, and Imbolc, when we anticipate the first stirrings of spring. For many, it is a long, dark, cold month, but one that allows us to turn our focus inward and to prepare for the journey that is the year to come. Like Janus, may we turn our faces forward with hope and youthful enthusiasm.

Deborah Blake

January 1
Wednesday

4th ♑

New Moon in ♑ 6:14 am

Color of the day: Yellow
Incense of the day: Marjoram

New Year's Day – Kwanzaa ends

The Dragon Bowl

Dragons represent success, growth, and the universe. They embody a powerful mystical force manifested on the physical plane. This is particularly true of Eastern dragons, with their more positive connotations, and of Western dragons, with their savage reputation. Which you prefer is up to you.

Today is an auspicious time to work magic for success, as this will carry throughout the coming year. For this spell you will need a glass goldfish bowl, a dragon figurine, and some symbolic treasure. The treasure can be golden coins, glass gems, pearly beads, ceramic eggs, or whatever represents achievement and abundance to you. Put the dragon inside the bowl, surrounded by the treasure, and then chant:

Look inside the dragon's lair;

See the treasure gathered there.

With this spell I charge and bless

All these things to bring success.

Keep the dragon bowl somewhere you can see it as a reminder of your achievements.

Elizabeth Barrette

NOTES:

January 2
Thursday

1st ♑

☽ v/c 6:12 am

☽ → ♒ 12:03 pm

Color of the day: Crimson
Incense of the day: Nutmeg

A Winter Cleansing Spell

The holidays are over and your routine is returning to normal. This is the perfect time for a ritual cleansing to banish any negative energy you may have hanging around.

Select a day when you'll be alone for a while. You'll need three straws from your broom, a bayberry-scented candle, and two short pine branches. Light the candle and, if you wish, say an affirmation for protection over it. Singe the tips of the broom straws—you don't want them to burn, you just want them to smoke. Walk around your home as you carry the straws. Begin and end in the east. Pay special attention to doors, windows, fireplaces, or any opening. After this, you may now burn the straws in a fireplace or your cauldron. Next, lay the two small pine branches over each other to form the shape of a solar cross, and burn. Let the candle burn out.

James Kambos

January 3
Friday

1st ♒

☽ v/c 8:47 pm

Color of the day: Pink
Incense of the day: Yarrow

Joys and Sorrows

Many Pagans belong to the Unitarian Universalist (UU) church, known for its open-door policy to seekers of all persuasions. The UU church devotes part of its weekly service to "joys and sorrows," a time for participants to reflect on their lives and those of their families and communities.

Set aside time on the first Friday of each month for your own joys and sorrows. Work at your ancestor altar, or light a candle. Begin by speaking aloud the names of your beloved dead, honoring them. Next, speak aloud your sorrows. What difficulties or challenges are in your life right now, or in the lives of your loved ones? Give voice to these and, if you wish, appeal to your own deities and patrons for assistance. Finally, speak aloud your joys, hopes, and dreams, pondering the wealth of your life for some time before offering thanks and extinguishing the candle.

Susan Pesznecker

January 4
Saturday

1st ≈

☽ → ♓ 11:58 am

Color of the day: Blue
Incense of the day: Pine

Crossroads Tarot Spread

In many traditions, Hecate, goddess of the crossroads, has associations with Saturday. To get the new calendar year off to a fresh start, here is a Hecatean-inspired tarot spread to help you decide which way to turn at a personal crossroads in your life.

Think of a decision you are faced with in your life that you need some assistance in making. Think of what your three most obvious options/courses of action are for this situation. Now, draw one tarot card for each possible option. Arrange the cards at a slight angle to each other, as if forming a three-way crossroads. These cards represent the different directions you can take at the crossroads you are standing at.

Carefully analyze the cards you have drawn and, if needed, ask for Hecate's guidance in making your decision.

Blake Octavian Blair

 January 5
Sunday

1st ♓

Color of the day: Gold
Incense of the day: Eucalyptus

National Bird Day

If a bird is your spiritual guide, today is the day for celebrating your connection. Offer up a few words of gratitude for their protection and direction. Purchase a new bird feeder or two. Stock up on fresh seed, or look into a different type of feed. Clean and refurbish existing feeders and bird baths.

If you are still seeking a guide, perhaps a bird is also seeking you. Consider it a sign if you have repeated experiences with certain birds. Numerous books and websites enable thorough research, as do natural history museums and wildlife habitats. The possibilities are endless. Look beyond the wise owl and the peaceful dove. Every bird holds symbolism and power—even if it is special to you alone.

Emyme

January 6
Monday

1st ♓

☽ v/c 4:44 am

☽ → ♈ 2:45 pm

Color of the day: Lavender
Incense of the day: Narcissus

Resolution Momentum

It's the first Monday, the first full week of work or school this year. If you made resolutions, you are at that point where some of the more difficult ones are taking a toll on you. Your body may be tired from a new lookout on exercise, or it may be planning a revolt from a lack of sugar, nicotine, or caffeine.

Today is a great day for an extra boost to keep yourself headed in the right direction. As you are getting ready to start your day, take a moment for the following chant:

New year, new day,

New strength, new way.

New life, new me,

So mote it be.

Chant it to yourself throughout the day whenever you need a pick-me-up of strength.

Kerri Connor

January 7
Tuesday

1st ♈

Second Quarter 10:39 pm

Color of the day: Red
Incense of the day: Cinnamon

Bring Me Money

Need to draw more wealth in your direction? Try this simple spell that makes use of Monopoly money. If you don't have a Monopoly game that you can raid for a few $500 bills, try doing an Internet search, where there are sites offering similar printable money. You will also need some good patchouli oil. (Good doesn't have to be expensive, but if it doesn't smell like dirt, it's not the good stuff.)

By the light of a green candle, lightly trace an emblem representing money onto the backs of three $500 Monopoly bills. Allow the oil to dry and then hold each bill above the candle, charging it to bring more money your way. Afterward, place them in your wallet, visualizing it full of greenbacks. (If you have your own business, you could also place the bills in your register drawer.)

Laurel Reufner

January 8
Wednesday

2nd ♈

☽ v/c 11:22 am

☽ → ♉ 9:24 pm

Color of the day: White
Incense of the day: Lavender

A Blessing for Art

It is a good idea to bless things that you create yourself, whether it's a painting, a sculpture, jewelry, or a scarf. When you take various ingredients and join them into a new creation, you are giving a new "life" and purpose to those ingredients. Blessing them in their new function is a good way to make sure all the parts are aligned as one, similar to how we charge charms, oils, etc., to align everything with our magical goal.

To cast this spell, hold the new item, or place your hands on it if it is too big to hold, and send energy into the item while speaking this chant:

Here I did shape with my own two hands,

And give form to these joined strands.

Idle bits fused in purpose and in art,

New life granted; a clean, fresh start.

Michael Furie

 ## January 9
Thursday

2nd ♉

Color of the day: Purple
Incense of the day: Balsam

Computer Cleanup and Protection

The holidays are over and the decorations are down, and now it is time to clean up your computer.

Be sure your virus protection is up to date and your subscription is current; if not, it's time to purchase the new anti-virus software of your choice. Make sure your files are backed up, because it is not a matter of *if* your computer will die, but *when.*

Also, be sure to clean your computer. Open it up and get all the dust bunnies that will block your air flow and cause the machine to overheat. Remove paper, dirt, dust, and anything else that may be blocking the air vents. Clean inside and the outside of the air vents. If you don't know how, seek professional help. Make a pentacle with protection oil on your tower and/or laptop covers.

Ask the Gods for special protection for your data. Keep it safe and secure.

Boudica

January 10

Friday

2nd ♉

Color of the day: White
Incense of the day: Orchid

Dream a New Dream

With the energy of the waxing moon and the newly turned waxing year, remember that you can refine or change the direction you're heading in life. Light a dark blue candle that you've dressed with lavender oil, and enter a meditation on your life's path. If you have an ambition or interest you've never pursued, remind yourself that now is a good time to start. If you're already on a career path, remind yourself that you can accomplish any goal you set for yourself within that career. Chant:

I am finding the path right now and right here,

I have the faith in myself to believe

The future is bright, right action is clear,

I'm pursuing what's mine, I'm living the dream!

Take a piece of flying wish paper, if you like, and write your dream on it. Then light it and send it to the stars!

Thuri Calafia

January 11

Saturday

2nd ♉

☽ v/c 5:58 am

☽ → ♊ 7:26 am

Color of the day: Brown
Incense of the day: Patchouli

Out, Out, Bad Spirits!

In Scotland, the tradition of "burning the clavie" is practiced today. A half barrel is filled with tar, lit on fire, and carried around town to get rid of evil spirits. Today is also the Christian anniversary of the baptism of Jesus.

Whether you use fire, water, or another element, clear, do a spell to cleanse, and bless. Mindfully clear the bad spirits from your home, self, and life with any of these easy techniques.

Use fire to smudge your house and self with sage (clearing) and sweet grass (blessing). Soak in a bath with Epsom and sea salts to cleanse and neutralize energy. Anoint with jasmine (healer of broken hearts) or rose (abiding love) essential oil. Using both fire and water, a diffuser broadcasts essential oils throughout your house. Use tea tree or rosemary oil to kill off cold and flu bugs. Out, out, bad spirits!

Dallas Jennifer Cobb

January 12
Sunday

2nd ♊

☽ v/c 4:33 pm

Color of the day: Orange
Incense of the day: Almond

home Peace Blessing

During and after the Yuletide, the home is overflowing with a general barrage of "stuff." This includes items from gift-giving, boxes, wrapped paper, ribbons, Yuletide decorations and altars, and perhaps even extra relatives. Here is a simple spell to reintroduce a little grounded peace and flow back into the home.

Stand at what you consider the hearth to be, and bless and consecrate a white taper candle there by simply grounding and centering, drawing up power from the earth and channeling it with intent into the candle. Light the candle and recite the following as the candle flame emanates the blessing into the home:

Blessings of a simple flow,

Of rest and peace in this home.

Blessings of the Holy Sun,

As I say, my will is done.

Gede Parma

January 13
Monday

2nd ♊

☽ → ♋ 7:25 pm

Color of the day: Gray
Incense of the day: Rosemary

heartwarming Beer Bread

Beer is an ancient beverage made of grains and one of the oldest beverages produced by humankind. Today is a traditional Druid festival of brewing, when they celebrated the craft of creating the blessed beverage. Brewing was a great way to preserve grains. To celebrate the nourishing properties of beer, look up a recipe for beer bread on the Internet; it's a quick bread and really easy to make. Mix the dry ingredients and, as you pour in the beer, use these words and your intention to enchant your bread:

Wheat and barley do the trick,

I make this bread of life right quick.

As this warm bread rises up,

We'll count our blessings and raise a cup!

Stir your bread batter clockwise with love in your heart. As it bakes, the bread will fill your home with warmth and happiness. Serve it with a hearty dinner.

Mickie Mueller

☽ January 14
Tuesday

2nd ♋

Color of the day: Black
Incense of the day: Ylang-ylang

A Good health Spell

This is a good spell to guard your health during the winter. You'll need cider, honey, and a cinnamon stick. In a small saucepan, combine a cup of apple cider and a tablespoon of honey. Gently heat while stirring occasionally. When heated through, pour into a mug and stir with the cinnamon stick.

Sit before a blazing fireplace, or light an orange candle. Gaze at the fire, then burn the cinnamon stick to purify the space. Slowly sip the warm cider, feel it cleansing your system. Inhale the scent of the cinnamon and say:

I end this spell, because I'm strong as iron and tough as nails.

Relax and unwind. This spell is an ideal bedtime ritual.

James Kambos

☽ January 15
Wednesday

2nd ♋

Full Moon in ♋ 11:52 pm
☽ v/c 11:52 pm

Color of the day: Brown
Incense of the day: Bay laurel

Carmentalia

The Roman goddess Carmenta, protector of women and children and patron of childbirth, was venerated on this day. The full moon in Cancer makes today doubly aligned with protecting and nurturing. So what would you like to nurture? Perhaps you'd like to nurture a project, a relationship, an animal companion, your child, or yourself. Whatever it is, obtain or create a pictured representation of it. Light a white pillar candle to Carmenta, and say:

Goddess Carmenta, I honor you.

Goddess Carmenta, I call on you.

Hold the picture to your heart, and close your eyes as you feel deep love for the object of your nurturance. Then place the image under the candleholder as you say:

Dear Carmenta, your love shines like bright, healing moonlight over all. Please share your power with me as I lovingly nurture _____. Thank you.

Tess Whitehurst

January 16
Thursday

3rd ♋

☽ → ♌ 8:00 am

Color of the day: White
Incense of the day: Myrrh

Spell to Bring Inspiration

Whether it's writer's block, painter's block, chef's block, or any kind of block that leaves us wondering what our next step should be, it is always a frustrating experience. I have found that when I am uninspired, it helps to get out of my head and ask for help from a higher power. One of the major deities who brings inspiration (particularly in Ireland) is the goddess Brigid (pronounced "Breedj"). To cast this spell, light a red candle (as Brigid is also aligned with fire), forget about whatever you are trying to create, and relax and go into a meditative state. When you are ready, call out to Brigid with this chant, and inspiration should arrive within twenty-four hours:

Goddess Brigid, hear my plea,

I offer up this gift of fire.

Unblock my creativity,

Fill my heart, renewed and inspired.

Allow the candle to burn for an hour, if safe.

Michael Furie

 January 17
Friday

3rd ♌

Color of the day: Coral
Incense of the day: Alder

Float Like a Butterfly, Sting Like a Bee

Today is the birthday of former heavyweight champion Muhammad Ali. The spell's title is how he described his boxing style— he danced about (floated) so that his opponent couldn't land blows: "His hands can't hit what his eyes can't see." When Ali's blows landed, however, they stung.

This spell makes you invisible to enemies. Should an enemy approach, and a confrontation is unavoidable, that's where your stinger comes in.

Surround yourself with a circle of white light, visualizing the great champion as your protector, or visualize the champion within yourself.

Impale a white candle with several pins (stingers). Hold a fan (representing a butterfly) in your hand.

Fanning yourself, recite:

Float like a butterfly, sting like a bee,
his/her hands can't hit what his/her eyes can't see.

(Change "hit" to "reach" or whatever applies.)

Dance about and recite your chant over and over until the candle flame burns past the pins.

Deborah Lipp

NOTES:

 **January 18**

Saturday

3rd ♌

☽ v/c 3:51 am

☽ → ♍ 8:23 pm

Color of the day: Black
Incense of the day: Rue

The Energy Within

Winter is the season of rest, when all the energy of Earth is held within and below, rather than expressed outwardly in green life. The world lies still and quiet beneath a blanket of snow, the trees bare, the animals hidden. Its power pools unseen.

This spell draws on that hidden energy. You will need an image of a bare winter tree, and a mirror—dark if you have it, though plain will work. Set the tree above the mirror to reflect as if in a pond. Imagine feeling the strength of elemental earth. Tap your fingers on the mirror and say:

Still water, silent ice,

Come knocking, once and twice.

Rapping, tapping, a sound

Of hidden power found.

Whenever you need to access the power of Earth, repeat tapping the mirror.

Elizabeth Barrette

January 19

Sunday

3rd ♍

☉ → ♒ 10:51 pm

Color of the day: Yellow
Incense of the day: Heliotrope

Energy Tea

Mix up a batch of this tea when you need a pick-me-up. Place 1 black tea bag, 1½ teaspoons chopped ginger (I use candied), 1 teaspoon dried peppermint, and a 4-inch stick of cinnamon in a heat-proof container. Add about 2 cups boiling water, and allow the brew to steep for 10 minutes.

Pour the resultant tea through a fine mesh strainer into a mug and let sit until it's cool enough to drink. I also like to add a squeeze of a lemon slice to the final mug. If you don't want to deal with the strainer, use a tea infuser or a small muslin bag.

Laurel Reufner

 January 20

Monday

3rd ♍

☽ v/c 3:55 pm

Color of the day: White
Incense of the day: Hyssop

Birthday of Martin Luther King Jr. (observed)

Carpe Birthday!

Today in the United States, we celebrate an important date: Martin Luther King Jr.'s birthday. And guess what? It's also my birthday! One's birthday is the most special day of the year—after all, it's the day we appeared on the planet, ready to practice intention, exert our will, and bend our little corner of reality.

Yes, many people eschew their birthdays, mostly out of wishing not to grow older. But I say, "Carpe Birthday!" Seize your birthday! Celebrate it, honor it, and be ridiculous about it. Take the day off from work if you can, and do something focused solely on you, something that's a bit of a luxury or a splurge. If you can't do this for yourself, who can you do it for? Take the day for yourself, and reflect on the magick and specialness you bring to the universe. Happy birthday, whenever it falls!

Susan Pesznecker

 January 21
Tuesday

3rd ♍

☽ → ♎ 7:43 am

Color of the day: Maroon
Incense of the day: Basil

Pardon Me

On January 21, 1977, President Carter pardoned all Vietnam War draft dodgers, so it's a day of forgiveness. Under the waning moon, let animosity wane. We'll use the image of a draft card for this.

Create an ID card for someone you haven't forgiven. Cut paper into a wallet-size card. Write the name, date of birth, and other facts. Add a description of the offense, such as "X slept with my boyfriend." Create a card for each person you wish to forgive.

Draft cards were burned, but forgiveness comes from the heart (element of water). Have a cauldron or bowl of cool water. Hold the card, visualize the person, and read the card aloud. Say three times:

I forgive you.

Place the card in the bowl. Stir it around, allowing it to disintegrate, and contemplate forgiveness until it has fallen apart. Do this for each card, and when done, say:

So be it.

Deborah Lipp

January 22
Wednesday

3rd ♎

☽ v/c 10:50 pm

Color of the day: Topaz
Incense of the day: Honeysuckle

Broaden Your Mind

We are three weeks into a new year, the time of year when many colleges are starting their spring semester. You don't have to attend official classes to try new intellectual pursuits. Make a trip to the library (or even search your library online) and start learning about something completely new and different to you. Browse the nonfiction sections and chant the following to yourself until a new, interesting topic grabs your attention:

Wisdom abounds in many ways,

What should I focus on

And learn today?

Our minds are made to be used. When we stop learning, we start dying a little on the inside. Give your mind new life and new topics to learn about to keep it happy and healthy.

Kerri Connor

January 23
Thursday

3rd ♎

☽ → ♏ 4:43 pm

Color of the day: Turquoise
Incense of the day: Carnation

Handwriting Day

This form of communication, though it may seem destined to become outdated in the future, will always be in fashion. Mind to hand to pen to paper creates great energy. Few things hold more thought and emotion than a handwritten note or letter. Care and caution are advised before sending negative-laden missives. A grimoire obtains much power not just from the spells, but also from the owner personally writing those spells, whether in cursive or printing.

Incorporate this blessing into your spellwork today, or write your own:

From my thoughts,

By my hand,

With this instrument,

To this paper,

Universally sent,

Grant my request:

_____

As I write, so mote it be.

Emyme

January 24
Friday

3rd ♏

Fourth Quarter 12:19 am

Color of the day: Purple
Incense of the day: Cypress

Reviving Love

It's a new year and time to refresh your relationship with your partner. You may have spent the holidays with family and friends, but now the two of you are back on your own.

Share some private time with your partner and treat yourselves to something special—maybe just some time alone with your partner, or maybe dinner and…? Those cold winter nights suggest snuggle time and lots of warmth. This time of year we need to remember that we are special and we deserve to love one another, and you can start with your partner.

Tell your partner they matter, they are important, and you care. Your times spent together with that special loved one are precious moments you should not waste. Love yourself, love your partner, and make the most of your time together.

Goddess, teach me to love.
Let me share that love with
my "someone special."

Boudica

January 25
Saturday

4th ♏

☽ v/c 8:55 am
☽ → ♐ 10:13 pm

Color of the day: Gray
Incense of the day: Sandalwood

Discover Your Patron hero

Many of us regularly work with a patron god or goddess, but how about a patron hero? A personal hero has a story from legend, myth, or history that we can connect with, and the spiritual energy behind their story can help guide us on our journey through life.

Seek your personal hero through meditation. Sit quietly and meditate, visualizing a mirror before you. Step through it, into a room of people. Announce that you're looking for a kindred spirit, your patron hero. The host leads you to a table where a figure sits, with back toward you. When you take a seat, and you discover your personal hero is waiting for you, talk with him or her for a while. When you are ready, thank your hero and step back through the mirror. When you arise from your meditation, do more research on your hero and discover what secrets he or she has for you.

Mickie Mueller

January 26
Sunday

4th ♐

Color of the day: Amber
Incense of the day: Marigold

Closet Cleaning

Choose a closet that needs cleaning and reorganization. Take your time as you pull out each item, asking yourself if the item is still needed in your life. Make separate piles for the items you will keep and the ones you will give to charity. While doing so, think about what's in your inner closet. Is there a part of you that you keep hidden, stored away for a future time when you can be "you"? Ponder whether that's a useful attitude for you.

When the closet is completely empty, sweep it out, stating:

As I sweep away that which is no longer needed, so I sweep away doubt and uncertainty.

Sprinkle the closet with saltwater. Take a sip, reminding yourself that it's okay to be yourself now! Promise yourself that you will speak to someone safe about what you've been hiding. Be blessed.

Thuri Calafia

January 27
Monday

4th ♐

☽ v/c 5:02 pm

Color of the day: Silver
Incense of the day: Neroli

What Goes Around Comes Back Around

If someone is causing problems, filling your life with misery, this spell is an ethical means of derailing their negativity and returning it to them to make them stop.

Anoint a white candle and the back of a small mirror with an oil made of nettle leaves steeped in olive oil for a week. Charge the candle and mirror with white light. Hold the mirror, close your eyes, and visualize the person sending black energy toward you. See yourself holding up the mirror; see this energy bouncing back out of the mirror, transformed and sent back to the person as gray light. When you feel ready, light the candle and chant:

Fiendish storm unleashed my way, captured, bound, held at bay.

Stripped of hatred, turned to gray,

Reflected back unto its source,

And bound about them to block the force.

Bury the burned-out candle and the mirror in the ground.

Michael Furie

NOTES:

January 28
Tuesday

4th ♐
☽ → ♑ 12:04 am

Color of the day: White
Incense of the day: Geranium

Triple Soul Alignment

In various traditions of Witchcraft, we align the three souls. Most commonly you will find this practice in the Anderson Feri tradition. It is also practiced in Reclaiming and WildWood Witchcraft.

Ground and center. Breathe into your heart and head, and see a golden halo of light—your Talking Soul. Breathe a prayer of blessing into this soul. Breathe into the space between your navel and sex, and see a viscous red energy—your Shadow Soul. Breathe a prayer of blessing into this soul. Breathe up, down, and all around, and behold your God Soul. This blossoming star shines royal blue, and you open yourself to it. Breathe upward now with the intent of aligning your souls. Hold your head back, breathe aloud the syllable "ha," and then feel the alignment of your three souls in your heart. Breathe into and from this place. You are in alignment.

Gede Parma

January 29
Wednesday

4th ♑
☽ v/c 11:47 am
☽ → ♒ 11:33 pm

Color of the day: Yellow
Incense of the day: Lilac

Practice Peace

Today is the historical birthday of the Roman goddess Pax and her Greek counterpart, Eirene. Invoke them and practice peace.

Early in the day, find a quiet, safe spot in which to sit quietly. Get comfortable and breathe deeply. Slow your heart rate and breathing. Settle. As you inhale, say:

I am.

And as you exhale, sigh:

Peace.

Let the exhale carry away tension, anger, worry, and agitation. Begin afresh with the next breath. With each breath, feel more at peace.

Throughout the day, when you find yourself in conflict, in an argument, angry, or stressed, pause and breathe again, returning to peace. The great Mahatma Gandhi said, "Seek to be the change you wish to see in the world." Today, take it a step further and be the peace that you wish to see in the world.

Dallas Jennifer Cobb

January 30
Thursday

4th ♒

New Moon in ♒ **4:39 pm**

Color of the day: Green
Incense of the day: Mulberry

Introspective Knot Spell

The New Moon is a powerful time for introspection and an excellent time for working on things that deal with the shadow self. Here is a spell to help untangle some inner issues you may be struggling with.

You'll need to gather a piece of yarn, twine, or rope a few feet long. Pick three issues you would like to unravel and untangle to gain clarity on. Tie a knot in the rope for each issue. Make solid knots, but leave them loose enough so you will be able to untie them again.

Once you have knotted your rope, hold it in meditation and contemplate the various options you have for dealing with the issue at hand with each knot. Once you feel you have internally confronted and contemplated each issue, begin to untie each knot while reciting the following:

Knot of one, this issue be done.

Knot of two, this issue I undo.

Knot of three, this issue is history.

Bury or safely burn the rope.

Blake Octavian Blair

January 31
Friday

1st ♒

☽ v/c 11:45 am

☽ → ♓ 10:45 pm

Color of the day: Rose
Incense of the day: Vanilla

Chinese New Year (horse)

The Year of the Wood Horse

The wood horse is enthusiastic about new ways of doing things, and is exceptionally assiduous and lively. To align with this new wave of energy, create a simple altar with a wooden representation of a horse and some living bamboo in water. (Be sure to keep it out of direct sunlight and to keep the water fresh.) Light a stick of woodsy incense, or diffuse some woodsy essential oil (perhaps cedar, eucalyptus, or juniper).

Sit or stand comfortably near the altar with your spine straight, and feel rooted into the earth like a tree. Say:

Out with the old and in with the new,

I flow with the changes and stand for what's true.

Rooted deep and reaching wide,

I welcome this new cycle's tide.

Today and throughout the year, be alert to ways that you can streamline your routine and move toward your goals in efficient, focused, and satisfying ways.

Tess Whitehurst

NOTES:

F ebruary is a month of extremes. It begins with the sabbat of Imbolc,
has a romantic celebration of Valentine's Day mid-month, and, just to
keep us on our toes, ends with an extra day some years. February is a magic
in-between time when anything can happen. Often the most brutal of winter storms occur now, and even though we get caught up in the romance
of the middle of the month and the revelry of Mardi Gras, spring can seem
far away. But the light increases every day, and we should remember that
February is all about the light, possibilities, and the hope of new life to
come. Deities associated with the month are the Celtic goddess Brigid and
the Greek deities Eros and Aphrodite. Folks born in the month of February
are assigned the violet and the primrose. The violet's magical qualities
include faery magic and good luck and cheer, while the primrose has the
enchanting qualities of protection and love. The amethyst is the birthstone
for the month of February. A very popular stone with most magic users, the
amethyst's magical properties include protection from manipulative magic
and the power to enhance personal protection and your own spellcasting.

Ellen Dugan

February 1

Saturday

1st ♓

Color of the day: Indigo
Incense of the day: Ivy

A Way with Words

The *Oxford English Dictionary* debuted on this day in 1884. So, let's do magic for verbal skill. This can help you write, speak, or master a language. Words are associated with the element of air.

Get a beautiful piece of paper or parchment, and a feather or quill pen with blue ink. Burn cedar or sage. Choose a sentence that represents your goal, or use "I have a way with words."

Prepare your altar as a writing table, light the incense, and begin with deep, cleansing breaths.

Begin writing your sentence in a clockwise spiral from the center out. Write it over and over, without stopping. You are expanding your verbal skills outward into the world. (If you want, you can mark the center and the spiral lightly, in pencil, in advance.)

Fill the paper to the outer edges. Fold it up as small as you can and leave it on your altar.

Deborah Lipp

 February 2

Sunday

1st ♓

☽ v/c 11:35 am

☽ → ♈ 11:55 pm

Color of the day: Orange
Incense of the day: Hyacinth

Imbolc – Groundhog Day

Imbolc Prayer

The name *Imbolc* means "ewe's milk," and this holiday originally celebrated the time when the sheep herd increased. New lambs are born and the ewes come into milk in late winter. This represents the return of life.

Celebrate the day by giving thanks for all the things that sheep have given us. They grow wool for spinning into yarn and cloth. Their milk makes excellent cheese. Some people also enjoy lamb meat. You can wear wool clothes today or serve foods that are associated with sheep. Use this prayer for thanksgiving:

Sheep in the barn,

Woolly and warm,

We give our thanks

For all you form:

Fleece for sweaters

And milk for cheese,

Lambs that scamper

Quick as you please.

Elizabeth Barrette

February 3
Monday

1st ♈

Color of the day: Gray
Incense of the day: Lily

Singing Praises

Today is the feast day of St. Blaise, a martyred physician and bishop from Turkey, known for interceding in cases of throat illnesses and injuries, especially fish bones stuck in the throat.

In honor of St. Blaise, exercise your vocal cords. Open your mouth and sing. Imagine you have finally had a fish bone pulled out of your throat, and let your joy and gratitude sing out. Choose a favorite song that you may have known for a long time. It hardly matters what the words are or what the song is about. Just open your mouth and let the sounds of your soul rise up and out.

Sing along to your favorite tunes in the shower, where acoustics are great. Sing really loudly in the car, with windows rolled up. Wherever you are, celebrate St. Blaise and your throat. Put joy into singing, and feel the joy that singing brings.

Dallas Jennifer Cobb

February 4
Tuesday

1st ♈

☽ v/c 6:14 pm

Color of the day: Red
Incense of the day: Bayberry

Blessing with Earth: The Earth Jar

Bless yourself with the earth element. Walk outside with your bare feet on the earth itself. Feel the soil and the stone, that which is the body of our earthly mother herself. Make a point of walking barefooted in as many places as you can: yard, park, mountain, streamside, ocean beach, and vacant lot. From each place you walk, scoop up a small bit of soil or sand, and add this to a large jar—a one-quart canning jar works well. The contents of this jar now hold connection between you and each of the places you have walked.

When you need a blessing or consecration, stir the jar's contents well, then take a pinch and either sprinkle over your head or use it to trace a symbol on yourself, your altar, tools, etc. Feel the blessings of earth through this bond of contagious magick.

Susan Pesznecker

 February 5

Wednesday

1st ♈

☽ → ♉ 4:47 am

Color of the day: Topaz
Incense of the day: Honeysuckle

A Snow Spell

Snow is nature's purifier. This spell works gradually to weaken and eventually destroy a bad habit. You'll need a bowl of pure, fresh snow or crushed ice, and a piece of jute garden twine about one foot in length. Place the snow and twine in front of you. First begin to wrap the twine around your finger while thinking of the habit you wish to stop. Repeat this as long as you want—feel the negative energy being absorbed by the twine. Place the twine into the bowl of snow/ice and press it into the snow with your hand. Allow the cleansing proper-ties of the snow to work for you as it draws impurities away from the twine. Pour the snow and twine onto the ground. As the snow melts, the negativity will be cleansed by the earth, and as the twine decomposes, the habit will fade.

James Kambos

February 6

Thursday

1st ♉

Second Quarter 2:22 pm

☽ v/c 11:49 pm

Color of the day: White
Incense of the day: Clove

Start a New Habit

With the waxing moon in Taurus, it's a great day to start a new habit and to maximize the likelihood that it will stick. What habit would you like to start? Jogging in the morning? Eating more veggies? Finally writing your novel?

Cleanse an agate or jasper in sage smoke or running water and then empower it in sunlight or candlelight. Hold it against your lower belly with both hands, close your eyes, and visualize yourself engaging daily in this lovely new habit. Feel the sense of accomplish-ment that goes along with sticking to it regularly, and see/imagine/feel all the wonderful benefits. Also see and feel yourself adopting this habit with more ease than you believed pos-sible. Three times, say:

I commit. I follow through.
I succeed. As I will it, so it must be.

Go outside and bury the agate near the base of a strongly rooted tree.

Tess Whitehurst

February 7
Friday

2nd ♉

☽ → ♊ 1:44 pm

Color of the day: Purple
Incense of the day: Violet

Opening to the Flow of Abundance

Go outside at midday and reach up to the power of the radiant sun as you breathe, ground, and center. Draw down that golden light into your body. Even if you cannot see the sun, the light is still flowing down from the heavens. Soon you will feel as if the light inside might explode if you do not channel it.

Instead of releasing the light at once, gradually let it emanate from your pores until you are "dressed" in gold. Say aloud:

I open to the flow of abundance!

And it is so.

Gede Parma

February 8
Saturday

2nd ♊

Color of the day: Black
Incense of the day: Sage

Anti-Bully Zone

Help grow an extra layer of protection around your child's school—or any area school that worries you—with the help of candles and mirrors. You will need to create a circle using three pink (friendship) and three blue (protection) candles. In the center, place a mirror face up, with a green or white pillar candle sitting on top.

If there is anyone you specifically want to target for protection from bullying, write their name on a slip of paper and place it under the pillar candle. Light the central candle while stating your intent—wanting to protect said children from harm and bullying from their peers, or something to that effect. Proceed to light the outer circle of candles, envisioning friendship, protection, and understanding encircling the children of the chosen school(s). Take a few moments longer to meditate and visualize before letting the outer candles burn themselves out.

Laurel Reufner

February 9
Sunday

2nd ♊

☽ v/c 4:08 pm

Color of the day: Yellow
Incense of the day: Frankincense

Read in the Bathtub

Cleansing and purifying the body is integral to spellwork. Although this does not always require complete immersion in water, today encourages that very thing. Take extra time to clean the tub surfaces. Gather candles, music, and a beverage of your choice. Create a pillow for your head; be sure the towels and your robe are at hand. Relax into scented water. What to read? Peruse the latest Wiccan supply catalogue, revisit your favorite well-worn book on the Craft, or research a skill you wish to cultivate, such as divination or candle magic. Classic fiction, poetry, historical romances, modern chick lit, biographies, travel, and how-to manuals… nothing is off-limits. The point is to turn off the rest of the world for a little bit of time, and feed your mind and refresh your body.

Emyme

February 10
Monday

2nd ♊

☽ → ♋ 1:33 am

Color of the day: Lavender
Incense of the day: Clary sage

Flow with Change

On this date in 1962, musical artist Bob Dylan released his album titled *The Times They Are a-Changin'*. The album's songs spoke about a wide variety of important topics, including racism, civil rights, social and political discontent, and the need for progress and moving within the flow and energy of change.

Many people have a natural resistance to change, even if it is ultimately for their greater good. In the spirit of flowing smoothly with change, choose a smooth stone, such as tumbled clear quartz or polished river rock, and visit a local body of flowing water. Hold the stone between your hands and visualize the flowing water surrounding the stone. Visualize how you are like the stone. The flowing water flows just as the flow of change does. Throw your stone into the moving water as a declaration of releasing your resistance to change. So mote it be!

Blake Octavian Blair

February 11
Tuesday

2nd ♋

Color of the day: Black
Incense of the day: Ginger

Besom Spell for Home Protection

The besom, or Witch's broom, is a powerful tool for both cleansing and protection. In magical spring cleaning, after your home is physically clean, it is a good practice to magically sweep any bad energy out the door using your besom. In addition to removing negativity, laying a charged broom across the doorway at night can protect your home from intruders.

To charge the broom, hold it brush side up in both hands and send energy into it while saying this spell:

Sweep out evil, hold danger at bay.

Balanced in power, my Witch's broom.

Shield us from harm sent our way,

I charge you now to protect this home.

Lay the broom across the front doorway each night before you go to bed.

Michael Furie

February 12
Wednesday

2nd ♋

☽ v/c 5:51 am
☽ → ♌ 2:15 pm

Color of the day: White
Incense of the day: Marjoram

To Work a Spell That You Can Reverse at a Later Date

You have cast a spell you want to reverse. Though it is not always easy to accept, sometimes you have to live with the consequences of your actions. Reversing spells can be difficult, depending on what you have done and the amount of change you have caused. Proper planning can make the spell reversible if you are careful.

String knotting a spell is a good way to begin learning how to cast and uncast a spell. You work the spell by knotting your spell into the string. Tie one knot for intent; as you knot, state clearly the purpose of the spell. Then tie one knot for success as you speak the expected outcome of the spell. And tie one knot to seal the spell. To undo the spellworking later, unknot and speak the spell in reverse order. Then burn the string.

Boudica

February 13
Thursday

2nd ♌

Color of the day: Crimson
Incense of the day: Apricot

Diagnosis

Sometimes we need healing, but sometimes we need a proper diagnosis. If you're in a situation that has medical professionals baffled, this spell can help.

Mark a cloth doll or poppet with the illness (if it's stomach pains, mark the stomach with an X). Be creative. It's traditional to make a healing poppet yourself and include healing herbs in the stuffing.

Cover the doll with a black cloth, representing ignorance.

Light a light-blue candle, representing knowledge.

Pointing your hands, wand, or athame at the doll, chant these words over and over:

Knowledge is power.

When the energy is at its peak, pull the black cloth away from the doll. Say:

All is known. All is seen.
Power has come.

Keep the poppet on your altar until the diagnosis arrives.

Deborah Lipp

February 14
Friday

2nd ♌

Full Moon in ♌ 6:53 pm
☽ v/c 10:13 pm

Color of the day: White
Incense of the day: Thyme

Valentine's Day

Be Your Own Valentine

As followers of a magical path, we know the ways of energy; that we cannot truly love another unless and until we love ourselves. Tonight, take some time to bathe yourself in moonlight! Feel the energy of the Goddess surrounding and engulfing you, and focus on your devotion to her. Let this feeling escalate into that of an adoration, just focusing on the feelings—no words are needed or desired in this time of Mercury retrograde. Let instinct and intuition rule; allow yourself to open up to all of that love, and then direct that same devotion and adoration toward yourself! After all, it was you who made the decision to come to this sacred road. Feel the energies of love and appreciation flow over you; flood yourself with adoration and moonlight. Afterward, treat yourself to a rose, and perhaps some champagne and chocolate, or a silky shirt. You deserve it!

Thuri Calafia

February 15
Saturday

3rd ♌

☽ → ♍ 2:26 am

Color of the day: Brown
Incense of the day: Magnolia

Find Truth in the Stars

Galileo, the Italian astronomer and visionary, was born on this day in 1564. He spent years of his life under house arrest, accused of heresy by the Pope upon reporting his celestial observations.

It may be a chilly night, but that makes stargazing even better. Bundle up, grab a cup of hot cocoa, and head out to spend a little time gazing up at the stars. Contemplate the conviction that it took for Galileo to challenge the ideas of his time about the cosmos, even through persecution. He found truths and insights in the night sky. What secrets do the stars have for you? Be sure to write them down in your Book of Shadows.

Mickie Mueller

February 16
Sunday

3rd ♍

Color of the day: Amber
Incense of the day: Juniper

Refresh and Refocus

Winter is long, and in the midst of the deepest, darkest part, it feels like lifetimes have passed since summer. Refresh your home and spirit with a cleansing spell. Clear out spiritual, emotional, and physical dust, and restore a clean gleam to your sacred realm.

I love the "top to bottom" method of cleaning and use a microfiber cloth, plus warm water with a few drops of lavender essential oil. Quickly wipe all glass surfaces—windows, mirrors, and stove doors. *My spirit is clear.* Shine all chrome and metal surfaces—stove, fridge, taps, and handles. *I reflect on the sacred.* Wipe broad, horizontal surfaces—tabletops, counters, shelves, and cabinets. *I am fully supported.* Use a wide mop (like the Cool Blue) to swish the floors, gathering up the dust. *My way is clear.* Empty dirty water outside. *I release confusion.* Return inside and enjoy. *All is clear, refreshed, and refocused.*

Dallas Jennifer Cobb

February 17

Monday

3rd ♍

☽ v/c 12:04 am

☽ → ♎ 1:23 pm

Color of the day: White
Incense of the day: Rosemary

Presidents' Day (observed)

Baking Up Togetherness

Those crazy Romans had a god or goddess for pretty much everything, and Fornax was the goddess of ovens. In February, she was celebrated with a three-day festival known as the Fornacalia. Help observe the last day of the Fornacalia and create some family togetherness/memories at the same time. There can be something quite soothing about baking bread together. It can also be a bonding experience to bake—or cook—with your family, especially the kids.

So break out one of your favorite recipes for quick bread, a yeast bread, or some other doughy, baked concoction and get to work. Just for the fun factor, I'd suggest this wonderful monkey bread recipe on FamilyFun .com: http://familyfun.go.com/recipes /monkey-bread-685023.

Laurel Reufner

February 18

Tuesday

3rd ♎

☉ → ♓ 12:59 pm

Color of the day: Scarlet
Incense of the day: Cedar

Clearing the Air

Today honors Tacita, a goddess of silence who protects against hateful, hostile speech. Often when we get upset or feel strongly about something, we don't always use a whole lot of tact in our communications. Tacita can teach us that sometimes it's better to simply say nothing at all and just let the moment pass.

What times in your life did you get worked up more than you needed to? Did blowing up really do you any good, or did it just make you feel worse? Getting hostile tends to lead to physical symptoms such as headaches, heartburn, or nausea.

Spend some time in silence today. Think about how different some conversations could be if you remember to remain calm and tactful. Sometimes biting our tongue may be the best, most peaceful route. If it really doesn't need to be said, don't bother saying it.

Kerri Connor

February 19
Wednesday

3rd ♎

☽ v/c 4:52 pm

☽ → ♏ 10:33 pm

Color of the day: Yellow
Incense of the day: Lilac

Yes, We Pray!

Some people have questioned whether or not Pagans pray, believing it to be a construct of patriarchal churches. But yes, we pray—and we should absolutely reclaim and glory in this important practice. The word *pray* comes from Latin roots meaning "obtained by entreaty." When we pray, we may simply seek to talk with our Gods and Goddesses, or we may entreat them—asking them for help, guidance, strength, etc.

Select a time of day for regular prayer—morning works well for many people. Light a candle and either speak what's on your mind spontaneously or repeat a prayer of your choice. Your prayer needn't be long, but it should be done mindfully.

Here's a morning prayer you might try:

Mindful now, I come to pray,

Here beneath the rising sun.

Guide me safely through the day,

Shielded 'til this day is done.

Susan Pesznecker

February 20
Thursday

3rd ♏

Color of the day: Green
Incense of the day: Jasmine

Honoring Connections

Relationships are what connect us to each other. They are strings of energy stretching from one person to the other. This is a type of magic that most people can sense. We call on it when creating new connections or strengthening those that already exist, or when we need support from someone else.

Today's working acknowledges relationships by representing them in the physical realm. For this you'll need different colors of cotton string, like red (romance), pink (friendship), green (relatives), blue (coworkers), purple (covenmates), and white (miscellaneous).

For each relationship in your life, cut a piece of string. Tie it around your wrist, saying the name of the person it represents. Then say this blessing:

Love and friendship,

Kin and kind,

Ever in my

Heart and mind.

Magic made and

Lives entwined,

Thus we honor

Ties that bind.

This can also be done as a group ritual.

                    Elizabeth Barrette

NOTES:

February 21

Friday

3rd ♏︎

☽ v/c 5:10 pm

Color of the day: Rose
Incense of the day: Rose

Enchanting a house Guardian

If you wish to charge an object and have it as a house guardian, take a small elf statue and place it on the fireplace mantle. (If you do not have a fireplace, you can hang a "kitchen witch" up in your kitchen.) Set a bowl of honey and a beeswax candle safely nearby. Ask the Goddess to bless your work, then light the candle. When the candle is lit, hold the statue or kitchen witch and send white light into it while chanting:

> Magical creature, charged with life,
>
> Protect this house from damage and strife.
>
> New little spirit, quick-witted, loyal, powerful, and true,
>
> In the name of the Goddess, I give form to you!
>
> Blessed may you be, I name you (state name), O mystic Fae,
>
> Guard this home in which you stay.

Breathe gently on the statue to "give it life." Pour the honey out onto bare earth.

Michael Furie

NOTES:

February 22
Saturday

3rd ♏

☽ → ♐ 5:12 am

Fourth Quarter 12:15 pm

Color of the day: Gray
Incense of the day: Patchouli

Out, Out, Damn Spot!

Is there something in your life that is lingering, clinging to you, that you really wish would just leave? Try this spell to banish this enduring annoyance, habit, or pattern.

On a piece of white paper, create a sigil of what it is you are banishing by writing it out in full and then crossing out all the vowels and repeated consonants. Then create one single image (sigil) out of the remaining letters. Inscribe this sigil in red ink onto black paper.

Ground and center, and align. Burn the black paper and chant:

Out, out, damn spot!

Out, out, I say!

My power as Witch

Will work my Way.

This thing is gone,

And I am free!

My power as Witch

Liberates me!

Gede Parma

 # February 23
Sunday

4th ♐

Color of the day: Gold
Incense of the day: Almond

Success Oil

Here is my recipe for success oil. Use it on business cards and resumés and for attracting money.

Supplies:

A bottle

Sunflower oil

Essential citrus oils (lemon, orange, or grapefruit, or a combination—the zest of these can be used as well)

Gold flake powder

Small piece of citrine

These are sun products—symbols of success. Add sunflower oil to the bottle, leaving space at the top. Add drops of citrus oil, blending till it smells "right" to you. I use up to 10 drops of essential oil per half cup of sunflower oil, depending on how strong I want to make the batch.

Add just a pinch of the gold flake powder. Remember, the powder will settle, so be sure to include the citrine as another accelerator and

a "shaker" to mix the gold powder with the other oils. Add your intent to finish.

Boudica

NOTES:

 February 24

Monday

4♏ ♐
☽ v/c 4:25 am
☽ → ♑ 8:50 am

Color of the day: Silver
Incense of the day: Hyssop

Seeds of Change Spell

At this time of year, we look forward to spring and all the things we hope to do. Most of us want to make changes in our lives as spring approaches. This spell will help remind you of what you want to do, even after you've performed the spell.

You'll need a brown candle and a package of garden seeds that like to be planted in cool weather. Dill, lettuce, spinach, and California poppies are a few ideas. Light the candle. Place your hands on the package of seeds, then close your eyes and think of the change you wish to make. Open your eyes, and slowly slide the seeds toward the candle. Snuff out the candle.

At the proper planting time, sow the seeds outdoors. As you tend them and watch them grow, keep working on your goal. As your plants grow, your wish will come closer to fruition, too.

James Kambos

 February 25

Tuesday

4th ♍ ♑

Color of the day: White
Incense of the day: Basil

Plum Blossom Tea Ritual

Today the Plum Blossom Festival is celebrated at Kitano Tenman-gu, a Shinto shrine in Kyoto, Japan. It commemorates the deified scholar Sugawara no Michizane, to whom the shrine is dedicated, with tea cere-mony. Because Michizane is popular-ly petitioned for success in academic pursuits, you might perform this tea ceremony to support your studies or other self-improvement endeavors (such as exercise or career-advance-ment goals).

Light a white or burgundy candle to Michizane near a small bouquet of plum blossoms (or an image of them if they are not readily available). Make a pot or cup of green tea, and mindful-ly drink it alone or with one or more companions. Pay close attention to the taste of each sip as you carefully consider your goals. Allow the ener-gizing vibration of the plum blossoms to fuel your inspiration and motiva-tion to succeed. Visualize/imagine/feel yourself reaching your goals, and know that this is your destiny.

Tess Whitehurst

 February 26

Wednesday

4th ♑

☽ v/c 5:51 am
☽ → ♒ 9:55 am

Color of the day: Brown
Incense of the day: Bay laurel

Successful Communication

Mercury, Wednesday's planetary ruler, is intimately tied with communications. We're approaching the tail end of a Mercury retrograde, which is notorious for making clear communication tricky. Time for a charm to promote clarity in your communication endeavors! Gather a clear quartz crystal point and a yellow ribbon or strand of yarn. After cleans-ing your crystal under running water or in a bit of incense smoke, take your ribbon and tie it, knotting it three times, around the quartz point while reciting:

Color of yellow, illuminate my intent.

Crystal of quartz, magnify my clarity.

By knot of three, so mote it be!

Hold the completed charm to your third eye, and focus on your intent once again. Then carry the charm on your person, clearing and reprogram-ming it as needed.

Blake Octavian Blair

February 27

Thursday

4𝄐 ≈

Color of the day: Purple
Incense of the day: Nutmeg

Equirria

Today we celebrate Equirria, the ancient festival of chariot races to honor Mars. It is the "dead" of the winter, but spring is on the horizon, less than one month away. Rally the forces of hope and light. Be a warrior, like Mars, and fight through the cold and the bleak, or the boring and the dreary. Book a ride at a local stable—even the most urban of areas have them. If you are an equestrian, you know how soothing a ride can be. Or consider a visit to a farm, bearing treats of apples or carrots. (Be sure to ask permission!) If these options are not available to you, place a small figurine or picture of a horse on your altar, and ask Mars for his blessing:

As in a chariot race,

I ask your blessings, great Mars.

Grant me power, courage, and stamina,

Bring the light of spring to this dark winter.

Emyme

February 28

Friday

4𝄐 ≈

☽ v/c 5:55 am

☽ → ♓ 9:53 am

Color of the day: Pink
Incense of the day: Mint

De-Labeling Ourselves

On this last day of Mercury retrograde, under the last sliver of the waning moon, the Crone's Sickle, it's a good time to discard some of the labels we've been plastered with. Write all of those "messages" you've been bombarded with on small pieces of paper, then safety-pin or tape them to an old t-shirt and put it on.

Cast your circle calling your most powerful gods and guardians to help you. Focusing on the power of the Crone's Sickle, remove and then read each label out loud, stating that this is no longer (or never was!) true of you, and then burn each label in the flame of a black (for the Mystery) or dark blue (for deep emotions) candle. When all the labels have been burned, burn or bury the t-shirt, and be free. Plan to move forward when the moon turns.

Thuri Calafia

March

March is a time of the year when anything can and does happen. Some days are warm. You can soak up the sun and feel the promises of the summer stirring in your heart. Other days an icy wind can chill you and have you clutching a jacket close. It's enchanting to watch daffodils and crocuses push their way up, proving that once again, life has reclaimed the earth. It's an exciting time of change, heralding the vernal equinox. Trees have begun to produce small, smooth buds on their bare branches, and nature is really pushing those buds to swell and pop forth with blossoms of all kinds, showering the world with color. I always think of March as nature's last snooze under the warm blankets in the morning, and now she must rise and face the shining day! It's a month all about breaking inertia, new beginnings, and potential. Magically, this is the perfect time to begin a new project and to take advantage of all the new growth energy in the air. It's also a perfect time to cast a spell to clear out what no longer serves us. Use the March winds to blow away the old, dead leaves and reveal new life.

Mickie Mueller

March 1
Saturday

4th ♓

New Moon in ♓ 3:00 am

Color of the day: Blue
Incense of the day: Sage

New Moon Ritual – Assessing a New Project

Your project should be clearly stated on paper and outlined in detail before you start this ritual. Pay attention to specifics, as Mars turns retrograde today. You should have a jar candle for seven days.

Place your project outline on your altar. Sprinkle it with some success oil you made (see February 23), and ask for blessing on the project from your Gods and light the candle.

Follow your outline for the project, getting it started during the next seven days. Your outline provides the steps to follow; you should do as many of the steps as possible—pricing supplies, gathering information, and putting the initial process into motion—so that the project is in the works by the full moon. This ritual enables you to start the process and judge its feasibility and potential for success by the full moon.

Boudica

March 2
Sunday

1st ♓

☽ v/c 6:04 am

☽ → ♈ 10:40 am

Color of the day: Amber
Incense of the day: Marigold

holy Well/Spring Blessing

If you are fortunate enough to have a well or a natural spring on your property and would like to bless and consecrate it as a place of magic and charge the waters with healing energy, the following spell can be used.

Go to the well or spring and hold your hands over it and try to feel the natural power of the place, that delicate hum of Mother Earth. When you feel it, ask the Goddess to help strengthen and empower the spirit of place so that the well will continue to grow in power. When you feel ready, chant this spell to bless and charge the water:

Bubbling up from Mother Earth,

Waters of life and untold worth,

Heal and cleanse, blessing ensure,

Whatever you touch shall now be pure.

Magical well, sacred space, I connect to you,

Ancient spirit of place.

Blessed be.

Michael Furie

March 3
Monday

1st ♈

Color of the day: Ivory
Incense of the day: Narcissus

Peach Blossom Day

Today is Peach Blossom Day. The peach tree represents love, affection, harmony, and peace. Furthermore, peaches are the fruit of immortality. They promote health and longevity. There is also the legend of Peach Blossom Spring Village, a place in which enlightened people gather to live a peaceful life away from the complications of the ordinary world.

This spell strengthens the heart and enhances love for all beings. To cast it, you will need a vase with several twigs of peach blossoms. If you can't find live peach blossoms, silk ones will do. Place the vase on your altar and use it as a focus. Then recite this invocation:

The heart is the center of love,

Love for all living creatures.

The fragrance of the heart

Is the perfume of peace.

Let my heart open like

A peach blossom,

Releasing the energy

Of love and peace.

Elizabeth Barrette

NOTES:

March 4
Tuesday

1st ♈

☽ v/c 12:31 pm

☽ → ♉ 2:12 pm

Color of the day: Black

Incense of the day: Ylang-ylang

Mardi Gras (Fat Tuesday)

Fat Tuesday Prosperity Ritual

Mardi Gras, or Fat Tuesday, is a traditional celebration of excess before entering the austerity of Lent. The moon's aspects make today perfect for magically riding this wave of indulgence with a high-spirited prosperity ritual that involves going all out with the luxuries. For example, you might plan a decadent meal, get all the ingredients for your favorite mixed drink, take a bubble bath, put on the satin pajamas, and burn the expensive incense.

Once you've planned and assembled the items you'll need, take a moment before partaking of the splurges to light a deep red candle, take some deep breaths, center your mind, and say:

With the fiery light of Mars,

The waxing fullness of the moon,

And the growing power of the Sun,

I now align.

I am rich. I have plenty.

My cup overflows.

My wallet swells.

Whatever I need, I have.

Luxury is my natural state.

Then enjoy!

Tess Whitehurst

NOTES:

March 5
Wednesday

1st ♉

Color of the day: White
Incense of the day: Lavender

Ash Wednesday

Come to Me Business Prosperity Powder

Lure more paying traffic to your place of business with this magic powder. Grind equal parts of basil, cedar, thyme, and ginger with a mortar and pestle or a coffee grinder. Add one packet of Stevia sweetener to make your business even more appealing. Finally, mix the combined powders with four parts ground cinnamon to both make it go further and add some heat to the mix.

This powder is very easy to use. If possible, start just outside your doorway, sprinkling the powder lightly, and work your way inside as though you were laying a trail of breadcrumbs for potential customers to follow. You don't need to sprinkle it more than three feet inside your door. If possible, leave the powder down for an entire business day—you'll need to use the powder lightly to do this.

Laurel Reufner

March 6
Thursday

1st ♉

☽ v/c 8:55 am

☽ → ♊ 9:37 pm

Color of the day: Crimson
Incense of the day: Myrrh

Paying It Forward

Spring is almost here, and Thursday is for generosity. Put these together and it's time to clean and help someone out. As you sort belongings, remember it's the perfect time to clean out old ideas, too. What stops you from doing more for others? What ideas do you need to get rid of to be able to help people in the future? Use the following as a meditation or journal exercise:

Why do I help the people I do?

Do I hold back from providing assistance to others?

Do my prejudices affect who I help?

Do I make excuses?

Do people discriminate against me?

How would I feel if people treated me the same way?

If you have prejudices, put them aside. Everyone has hard times at some point in their lives. Give people a hand up when they need it. Someday you may be the one reaching out for help.

Kerri Connor

March 7
Friday

1st ♊

Color of the day: Coral
Incense of the day: Orchid

The Empress as Project Manager

The nurturing and loving energy of the Empress of the tarot's major arcana resonates with Friday's vibrations. Before beginning work for the day, pull the Empress card from your tarot deck. Contemplate a project or goal you are in the process of completing. Allow the nurturing and motherly energies of the Empress archetype to be your project manager. Draw two more cards, laying them directly beneath the Empress, asking her for guidance on how to best move forward with, and finally reach, your project's goals. What advice does she have for you?

Journal about your results and your new proposed plan of action. What steps will you take? Will you continue on the same path? Take a new direction? Draw more cards for clarity as needed.

Blake Octavian Blair

March 8
Saturday

1st ♊

Second Quarter 8:27 am

Color of the day: Gray
Incense of the day: Rue

Mother Earth Day

Today is Mother Earth Day, a festival that's celebrated in China. This is considered the birthday of the earth as a mother goddess. One of the ways celebrants like to recognize the Earth Mother's special day is by burying gifts for her in the ground. Choose whatever you wish: a coin, a stone, a flower, or even a handful of fertilizer! Dig a small hole and sit quietly on the ground and thank Mama Gaia for all the life that she supports, including your own. As you place your gift to her in the hole, say:

> Blessed be, my Mother Earth,
>
> I celebrate your very birth.
>
> I offer this gift, a little token,
>
> With gratitude this spell is spoken.

Use your hands to push the soil back over the gift. Meditate on the earth as a goddess, nurturing all life with her body and giving endlessly to all her children.

Mickie Mueller

NOTES:

March 9
Sunday

2nd ♊

☽ v/c 3:53 am

☽ → ♋ 9:33 am

Color of the day: Gold
Incense of the day: Eucalyptus

Daylight Saving Time begins at 2:00 am

A Wishing Tree Spell

A "wishing tree" is a tree that you bond with, and you can use it to enhance your spellwork. Select a tree first. It must appeal to you for some reason. It may be anywhere—in a park, your yard, or a forest. Just be sure you can get to it easily. When you find it, give thanks by pressing a penny into the soil near its trunk and say:

I give thanks for your friendship,

By pressing this coin into the ground.

I declare, from your root to crown,

We are now bound.

To make a wish come true, tie a small red ribbon to a branch as you focus on your wish. After asking the tree for permission, you may occasionally use parts of the tree in your spells, such as a leaf or a bit of bark. And now you have a wishing tree.

James Kambos

March 10
Monday

2nd ♋

Color of the day: White
Incense of the day: Lily

The Tintinnabulation of the Bells

In times past, church and town bells rang out to mark certain parts of the day, times for prayer, and more. Some cultures still use bells to signal these practices, the tintinnabulation sounding far and wide, reminding people of their obligations. Today, the bell is often overlooked as a magickal tool, but reclaiming its power will add a bright spot to your magicks.

Purchase a small bell: be sure to test several until you find one with a pleasing ring. Charge the bell in full cycles of sun and full moon, then consecrate it with all four elements, dabbing it with saltwater and passing it through the smoke above a burning candle flame. Use the prepared bell to mark sacred space or occurrences, ringing it to signal the start and end of prayer, meditation, ritual, or gatherings. Keep it on your altar space when not in use.

Susan Pesznecker

March 11
Tuesday

2nd ♋

☽ v/c 3:50 pm

☽ → ♌ 10:09 pm

Color of the day: Maroon
Incense of the day: Ginger

Choosing Seeds

As planting time approaches in so many regions, it's time to focus on inner growth. Purchase some tiny crystals for this spell. Cleanse them in saltwater, then cast your circle. Taking up each small "seed" crystal in turn, ponder an aspect of personality or growth that you wish to plant within. Allow the idea to grow in your mind, and let yourself see all the way through to that idea's completion. Focus your energy and fire it into the crystal, programming it with the energies you've conjured. Seal the spell in the crystal with some oil, repeating this process with all the ideas you wish to grow in yourself. Help yourself to some hearty cakes and wine, grounding the energies. Afterward, "plant" the crystals in areas of your home that represent the areas of your life you've planted the seed in, and be blessed.

Thuri Calafia

March 12
Wednesday

2nd ♌

Color of the day: Yellow
Incense of the day: Marjoram

A Lovers' Feast

This is a spell for lovers to indulge and revel in the making of love.

Together, create a feast of aphrodisiacs (like strawberries, champagne, and dark chocolate) and bless all of the food and drink. Decorate the room, and create an altar to either one or many love and sex deities/spirits. Place some of the blessed feast on a smaller plate onto the altar as an offering.

Light a red candle on the altar and say the following:

In the name of the powers of love and sex,

This holy temple we erect,

To be for us a blessed bower,

In this time and in this hour.

Feed each other the blessed feast and make love.

Gede Parma

March 13
Thursday

2nd ♌

Color of the day: Turquoise
Incense of the day: Mulberry

Looking Forward

With winter marching on, and spring soon to come, pause and look forward in the spirit realm. Herbs for this spell are available in most grocery stores. You will need fresh ginger and either lemon balm or lemongrass. Ginger aids psychic development and protection. Lemon balm enhances psychic powers and brings success. Lemongrass promotes clairvoyance and aids divination.

While water boils, grate a teaspoon of fresh ginger. *I reveal the goodness ahead.* Take a generous pinch of lemon balm or lemongrass and smell it. *Goodness flows toward me.* Place herbs and ginger in a mug, and add boiling water. While it steeps for five minutes, lean close to the cup, breathe in the fragrant steam, and look into the reflection. *I look to the future.* Let your eyes blur. Scry the future. *And now I see.* When you've seen images, sip the infusion, ingesting the magic. *The future is clear. Blessed be.*

Dallas Jennifer Cobb

 ## March 14
Friday

2nd ♌

☽ v/c 3:24 am
☽ → ♍ 10:17 am

Color of the day: Purple
Incense of the day: Cypress

National Pi Day – Albert Einstein's Birthday

Pi day is celebrated on March 14 because 3.14 are the most significant digits in Pi's decimal representation.

Today is also the 135th celebration of the birth of Albert Einstein. Are math and science the opposite of earth-based beliefs? Consider this: Pi is an irrational and transcendental number, meaning it will continue infinitely without repeating; and Einstein was a seeker and champion of the vast universe and all its mysteries.

Honor your irrational, transcendental, universal, and mysterious self with your favorite pie today. Add some light research into the life of Einstein on the side.

All religions, arts, and sciences are branches of the same tree.
—Albert Einstein

Emyme

March 15
Saturday

2nd ♍

Color of the day: Brown
Incense of the day: Magnolia

Beware the Ides of March

On this historic day of betrayal, do a spell to protect your home from the unknown. This will serve as an early warning system, alerting you to the presence of danger. The result should be that, if danger comes, you'll feel awareness of it; it will keep you from being caught off-guard.

Buy or make a wind chime with a pleasant sound. Anoint the chime with a protective oil, such as clove or juniper. Send energy into the chime, saying:

Warning bells keep me alert.
I am ever protected, I am ever safe.

Hang the chime near the front door of your home. You can hang the chime with protective herbs such as holly, bay laurel, or garlic.

If you live in an apartment and can't hang chimes in the wind, you can still do this spell using a small decorative bell at the front door.

Deborah Lipp

March 16
Sunday

2nd ♍

Full Moon in ♍ 1:08 pm
☽ v/c 1:08 pm
☽ → ♎ 8:46 pm

Color of the day: Orange
Incense of the day: Heliotrope

Purim

Blow That Bad Habit Away

Let's face facts: it's very hard to break a bad habit, regardless of the toll it may take on our lives. Make a commitment to yourself to do just that with just one bad habit with which you're currently wrestling. Draw on the power of a full moon to let this little spell help strengthen your resolve.

You'll need a small tray—even a picture frame will work—and some cornstarch. Dump enough cornstarch on the tray to cover the surface, and you're ready to begin. Look at the coating of cornstarch, and imagine that it's the residue of your chosen bad habit, coating your life. With a finger, write in the cornstarch any word that to you represents the bad habit. Now take your tray outside (a wide-open window might work), take a deep breath, and blow the cornstarch away into the air, visualizing your bad habit floating away with it.

Laurel Reufner

March 17

Monday

3rd ♎

Color of the day: Silver
Incense of the day: Neroli

St. Patrick's Day

Spell to Reveal hidden Truth

Since it has been proven that there were no snakes driven out of Ireland by Saint Patrick—that was merely a metaphor for (almost) driving out Irish Paganism—I feel that this day is an ideal time to work a spell to reveal truth that has been covered up by lies or distortion from others.

To cast this spell, light a white candle and burn an incense made of equal parts powdered deer's tongue, calamus, and licorice root on an incense charcoal, and meditate. Concentrate on what you want revealed while chanting:

Layers of gloom, obscure what's real,

The fog is swept and cleared away.

For ultimate good, I ask now, reveal!

The truth be known by light of day.

Once you have cast the spell, snuff out the candle and allow the incense to burn out. The next day, when everything has cooled, bury the spell remains in the earth.

Michael Furie

March 18

Tuesday

3rd ♎

☽ v/c 9:07 pm

Color of the day: White
Incense of the day: Cinnamon

Badge of Courage

Be courageous. Do one thing that requires you to be courageous. Long ago, kings and tribal chiefs had to be courageous and sacrifice their lives for the good of the people. Though you don't need to sacrifice your life, there are plenty of ways you can stand up for yourself that would take a bit of courage. Say this chant as loud as you want to build that confidence and to let your courage out in a roar:

I am strong, I am brave,

I am a master, not a slave.

I am tough, I am strong,

I know I'm right, I'm not wrong.

I stand for you, I stand for me,

I stand courageous for all to see!

This is a simple rhyme, but once you start speaking it loudly, you will feel the power swell inside of you. Let it burst out!

Kerri Connor

March 19
Wednesday

3rd ♎

☽ → ♏ 5:13 am

Color of the day: Brown
Incense of the day: Honeysuckle

Break a Spell Cast by Someone Else

It's obvious you did something to make someone angry. That person is not going to reverse the spell, so you will need to do it yourself.

For an un-hexing ritual, my recommendation is bathing with uncrossing oil and bath salts. Use a seven-day white candle anointed with vetiver oil (or a jinx-removing candle/oil) with the name of the person who cast the spell on you engraved into the candle. Burn incense of Low John Root (*Trillium grandiflorum*) and pine needles. You can also invoke your deity to help remove the hex. The best way to remove a curse is with a blessing—that the other person finds peace and moves on. Word your blessing according to your situation. Do this daily for all seven days till the candle is burned out.

Remember, if you brought this upon yourself, you will sustain some kind of backlash.

Boudica

March 20
Thursday

3rd ♏

☉ → ♈ 12:57 pm

☽ v/c 11:12 pm

Color of the day: Green
Incense of the day: Apricot

Spring Equinox – Ostara

Rubber Ducky Spell

The spring equinox marks the Pagan holiday of Ostara. It is a time of balance, when the light is slowly growing stronger.

This holiday represents rebirth and regeneration, when the world comes alive again after winter. Baby animals are born. Spring rain encourages plants to sprout and flowers to bloom. Ducks and ducklings appear among the famous symbols of this season. The stormy weather can bring danger, though, along with life-giving rain. Ducks represent the ability to sail serenely through challenges.

For this spell, you need a classic rubber ducky. Float it in a bowl of water on your altar. Meditate on the weather, in its positive and negative aspects. Then say this incantation:

No matter the storm,

Duck sails calmly on.

Wind blows and rain falls,

And then they are gone.

Gentle the storms with

The power of Duck.

Bring spring's renewal,

And hope and good luck.

Elizabeth Barrette

NOTES:

March 21
Friday

3rd ♏

☽ → ♐ 11:39 am

Color of the day: Pink
Incense of the day: Violet

Rekindle Your Passion

Sometimes we fall into a routine with our lover, even when the person is our soul mate. Everyday life can zap the passion right out of us. Spending some special time together can reignite that old passion and bring some good old-fashioned romance back into your life.

Carve a heart with your initials on one side of a red candle and your anniversary date on the other. Now charge the candle:

We fan the flame of passion strong,

Rekindling our love so long.

Bring clarity into our hearts,

Reminding us of our true love's start.

Have a bowl of fresh strawberries nearby. Feed your partner a strawberry and tell them one thing about them that you find attractive or recall a happy memory of your first year together. They should do the same with you. Repeat this process until the strawberries are gone, and let the evening progress as it will.

Mickie Mueller

March 22
Saturday

3rd ♐

Color of the day: Black
Incense of the day: Sandalwood

Clear the Pathway to Love

Of all the things in life, soul mate relationships can be both the most satisfying and the most trying. Some days you can feel blissful, and other days you can feel a million miles apart. This spell helps clear the invisible pathway between your hearts so that you can rediscover your compassion for each other and, in turn, your harmonious coexistence.

Cleanse two rose quartzes in running water for at least one minute, and then charge them in sunlight or candlelight for at least one minute. Sit comfortably and hold one crystal lightly in each hand. Close your eyes and see yourself standing across from your partner in the middle of a beautiful meadow. See both of your hearts as windows with shutters. See these shutters open and reveal blindingly bright suns. See a bridge of light form between your two hearts, nourishing each of you deeply and cleansing away roadblocks to understanding.

Tess Whitehurst

March 23
Sunday

3rd ♐

☽ v/c 6:40 am

☽ → ♑ 4:03 pm

Fourth Quarter 9:46 pm

Color of the day: Yellow

Incense of the day: Frankincense

For Clarity and Balance

No matter where we are in the world, we are close to the equinox. What a perfect time to invoke clarity and balance into our lives.

Find a place of peace and power, and breathe, ground, center, and align. With fine granules of frankincense, create a symbol(s) of clarity and balance before you. Charge these frankincense symbols with power by channeling life force at them with intent and precision.

Start to dance and clap while chanting "clarity" and "balance" over and over. When you feel the peak of power, release the energy into your own body. Ground.

Gede Parma

March 24
Monday

4th ♑

Color of the day: Gray

Incense of the day: Clary sage

Monday Mojo

For many of us, Monday mornings can be a bit of a drag as we try to garner the motivation to get the work week started. The energies of the ingredients in this simple mojo bag will provide an energetic boost to your motivation as well as a boost of invigorating freshness and calm to your mood.

Take a small square scrap of any material with a color or pattern that makes you feel cheerful, and place in it a carnelian stone and a teaspoon each of mint and lavender. Draw the edges up together and tie shut to complete the mojo bag. Keep it on your person or in your workspace, and when you need a boost of calm, fresh energy, take in the scent and energy of the mojo bag.

Blake Octavian Blair

March 25

Tuesday

4th ♑

☽ v/c 8:35 am

☽ → ♒ 6:39 pm

Color of the day: Red
Incense of the day: Bayberry

Terroir Altar

Terroir (pronounced tehr-WAH) is a French word referencing the natural environment in which a thing takes root. Organic farmers, vintners, hop growers, and other agriculturists believe that terroir imparts a certain flavor or character to the crop—hence the unique depth of flavor in a small-batch beer or a local wine vintage. We humans respond to terroir as well—we're shaped and "flavored" by the places in which we live our lives. Yet even as many of us honor our ancestors and patrons, we often neglect to pay homage to our ancestral lands.

Set up a terroir altar. Include photos—or even map sections—of the lands that contributed to your character. Add statues or representations of trees, or, if possible, include stones, sticks, bits of earth, or even vials of water from the actual locations. Honor your own terroir as you honor your human ancestors, and be thankful for these precious gifts.

Susan Pesznecker

 March 26

Wednesday

4th ♒

Color of the day: Topaz
Incense of the day: Lilac

Make a Prayer Stick

Prayer sticks are frequently used by shamans to heal the sick, to drive away evil, and as offerings to the Gods. At this time of year, plum trees come into blossom. Plum tree branches are highly favored for use as prayer sticks. Healing and protection are powers associated with plum tree wood.

To make your prayer stick, first obtain a branch from a plum tree, and bless it. Carve, decorate, or paint it as you wish. Use symbols and designs special to you, and concentrate on your magical intent as you decorate your stick. When done, decorate one end of your stick with feathers to help raise your wishes to the divine spirit. Bless your prayer stick during a new moon before use.

To use your prayer stick, hold it and think about your need. Lay the stick on your altar, or push it into the ground. The stick will direct your magical energy.

James Kambos

March 27

Thursday

4th ≈

☽ v/c 9:13 am

☽ → ♓ 8:10 pm

Color of the day: White
Incense of the day: Carnation

hilaria Cleansing Ritual

In ancient Rome, on this day, the goddess Cybele's likeness was washed in a brook after a dark and heavy series of rituals. Flowers were strewn about, and laughter chased away the gravity of the previous days.

Lift your spirits today, and transmute heaviness into joy, by performing this ritual. Draw a bath. In it, dissolve a half cup sea salt and a quarter cup baking soda. Then strew fresh blossoms and/or petals across the water. (Be sure they are nontoxic and non-irritating.) Stand above the bath and direct your palms toward the water as you say:

That which is dark now turns to bright,

That which is heavy, now feather light,

Like fog in the sun, all sorrow shall part,

And my spirits shall rise with the dawn of my heart.

Soak for at least forty minutes. Afterward, watch a funny movie, dance to happy music, or laugh with a friend.

Tess Whitehurst

 March 28

Friday

4th ♓

Color of the day: Rose
Incense of the day: Rose

To heal a Rift

Use the waning moon to heal a rift that keeps two people apart (one of those people may be you).

You'll need a square of blue or pink fabric, fabric paints or markers in colors representing each person, scissors, and a needle and thread.

Draw the two people on the square of fabric. Draw each in his or her color. They can be simple stick figures with name labels.

Cut the fabric so that the two people are separated. Put them on opposite sides of your altar. Say:

The rift wanes.

Then move the two pieces closer together.

Repeat this again and again until the pieces are almost touching. Say:

The rift is gone.

Now have the pieces touch.

With needle and thread, sew the fabric back together. Say:

It is done.

Fold the fabric and carry it with you until the full moon.

Deborah Lipp

March 29

Saturday

4♏ ♓
☽ v/c 9:44 am
☽ → ♈ 9:54 pm

Color of the day: Indigo
Incense of the day: Pine

Contemplating Communications

Take some time today to think about your communication style. Are there ways you could improve it? How well do you speak your truth? More importantly, how well do you listen? Allow the power of the waning moon, so close to the new, help you go deep into your own Mysteries. Take a bright blue candle (blue for the throat chakra), and carve it with symbols of communication, such as the rune Ansuz, a smiling mouth, a spiral, or whatever works for you personally. Dress the candle with mugwort oil (for psychic awareness), light it, and deepen into meditation. Ask yourself:

> How can I improve my
> communications with myself?
> With others?

Listen without judgment to the answers, allowing yourself to receive the messages of the Divine. Afterward, follow up by turning these messages into positive affirmations. Use this advice in all of your relationships, and watch them improve.

Thuri Calafia

March 30
Sunday

4th ♈

New Moon in ♈ 2:45 pm

Color of the day: Amber
Incense of the day: Hyacinth

hidden Treasure

With the second new moon in March, today is an auspicious time for a ritual to manifest hidden treasure.

Begin by writing: *Thank you for the blessing of _____.* Write what you seek to manifest—wealth, health, luck, or love. Be specific. Write as if you already have it. Look at the paper and say:

As the moon waxes, my blessings grow, both seen...

Fold the paper in half and say:

...and unseen.

Place it on your altar, saying:

Abundant treasures lay inside of me. The light of the moon illuminates these. Treasures hidden and waiting for me. So mote it be.

Whenever you pass your altar, repeat your thanks. The law of attraction will work with the waxing moon to help you find hidden treasure.

Dallas Jennifer Cobb

March 31
Monday

4th ♈

☽ v/c 4:07 pm

Color of the day: Lavender
Incense of the day: Hyssop

Borrowed Days of April

In the British Isles, the 29th, 30th, and 31st of March are said to be "borrowed days" from April. There are plenty of stories and legends of why the month of March asked for and received three extra days from April. It may be that the weather in March is often more like winter than spring. Or maybe some found it difficult to reconcile a month of thirty-one days following a month of twenty-eight days. Whatever the reasoning, these days are traditionally feared to be bad-luck days. Guard your luck by lighting four candles—one each in black, light blue, brown, and magenta.

Create your own spell incorporating the following phrases:

Negative out, positive in;

Away from dark, toward the light;

Cleansed, purified, changed.

(With thanks to D. J. Conway, *A Little Book of Candle Magic.*)

Emyme

April

There is so much going on in the month of April! There is April Fools' Day, and it's National Poetry Month. It's also the anniversary of the sinking of the Titanic and the opening of the first McDonald's. We celebrate the birthdays of Hans Christian Andersen, Leonardo da Vinci, Sherlock Holmes, and Daffy Duck. But what is April really all about? What is it that makes April special? April marks the real end of winter. Daffodils pop open and nod their yellow heads. Grass starts to recover from its frozen cover of snow. Trees bud, forsythia shows its yellow cloak, tulips display their lips, and the small animals—chipmunks, squirrels, rabbits, and other animals—wake up from their winter sleep. The promise of renewal is realized as the sun removes the icy chill from the air. Rain soaks the earth, prompting growth and preparing the flowers of the season. And we find ourselves shedding our winter coats on the first warm spring day. This is April!

Boudica

April 1
Tuesday

1st ♈

☽ → ♉ 1:20 am

Color of the day: Black
Incense of the day: Geranium

April Fools' Day –
All Fools' Day (Pagan)

April Fools' Trivia

While there are plenty of stories floating around about the origins of this April holiday, no one really knows how it started. What is known is that its celebration goes back hundreds of years and it shares similarities with even older celebrations the world over. This just goes to show how important it is to have a day where we can all act goofy. Acting silly helps a community let off steam and bond over shared laughter. It can also bring luck. Some folklore has it that pranks must be pulled before noon, or they will bring bad luck to the prankster. If you're "lucky" enough to get pranked, remember to take it in stride and maintain a sense of humor. Being good-natured will bring you good luck, while getting angry draws bad luck. Now go prank one another!

Laurel Reufner

April 2
Wednesday

1st ♉

Color of the day: Brown
Incense of the day: Lilac

Circle of Fire Amulet

Obtain a carnelian stone (ideally in jewelry), five red candles, and an altar pentacle. Cast a circle (or visualize yourself surrounded by a circle of power) and place the pentacle on the altar with red candles placed around it at the pentagram points. Sit in front of the altar holding the carnelian, close your eyes, and meditate. When you are centered, visualize the planet Mars and see red light shining forth from it and pouring into your third eye and through you, into the stone and candles. Open your eyes and set the carnelian in the center of the pentacle. Light the candles and chant:

Circle of fire, the power of Mars I wish to wield,

Fill this charm with your mighty light.

Blazing energy, protective shield,

Burn away danger, put evil to flight!

Allow the candles to burn for an hour before extinguishing them. Carry the stone always.

Michael Furie

April 3
Thursday

1st ♉

☽ v/c 2:43 am

☽ → ♊ 7:48 am

Color of the day: Purple
Incense of the day: Clove

A Breath of Fresh Air

The element of air relates to thought and communication. It begins the cycle of life with birth, and corresponds to east and dawn. Within the body, it rules the lungs and respiratory system. This element reminds us that we need clean air to breathe in the material world, as well as clarity in the mystical realms. For that, we need a little help from the element of earth.

This spell relies on a houseplant (a live one, not silk), such as an air fern or philodendron. Houseplants improve indoor air quality by removing impurities and exchanging oxygen for carbon dioxide. Place the plant in your window and say this incantation:

Seeds of hope and sprouts of birth,

Rise up from the womb of earth.

Stems of brown and leaves of green,

Make the air all fresh and clean.

Roots of earth and fronds of air,

Cherish both with loving care.

Elizabeth Barrette

April 4

Friday

1st ♐ ♊

Color of the day: White
Incense of the day: Yarrow

A Spring Garden Spell

This ritual purifies and draws fertility to the spring garden. After the garden has been tilled, kneel before the freshly turned earth. At your side, have a watering can filled with water, and mix in a few drops of vinegar. Also, to honor the Goddess, have a few slices of apple with you. Begin by crumbling a few handfuls of soil between your fingers and inhaling its earthy scent. Then begin to sprinkle the water/vinegar mix randomly over the soil—this acts as a purifier. To attract fertility and the blessings of the Goddess, press the apple slices into the soil. As they decompose over the growing season, they'll release their magical energy into the soil and all of your plants. End by saying:

As the season goes, my plants will thrive,

As the season goes, this spell is alive.

James Kambos

April 5

Saturday

1st ♐ ♊

☽ v/c 10:55 am
☽ → ♋ 5:40 pm

Color of the day: Gray
Incense of the day: Sandalwood

Nice to Meet You, Mnemosyne!

The word *memory* comes from Mnemosyne (NEM-oh-seen), Greek goddess of memory and mother of the Muses, nine goddesses who presided over the creative arts. Believing the Muses' powers were necessary to inspire acts of creation, starving artists in ancient times (poets, playwrights, musicians) invoked the Muses' aid in fashioning their works. You can do the same today, and also call on Mnemosyne for a memory boost.

One way to access deep levels of memory is to sit down with pencil and paper and "freewrite." Burn a candle or incense of cinnamon, honeysuckle, or rosemary. Visualize your central idea and, with it in mind, begin writing. Once you've started, don't stop! Keep writing whatever comes to mind—even if it veers off the original topic. Don't edit yourself and don't stop until there's nothing more to write: you'll be surprised at the depth of recollection. Thanks, Mnemosyne!

Susan Pesznecker

April 6
Sunday

1st ♋

Color of the day: Gold
Incense of the day: Juniper

Success in Court

The best and most effective magic for winning in court is sympathetic magic. The night before, burn a purple candle anointed with Little John to Chew oil. Or carry a spell bag with Little John to Chew root and a bloodstone. Put your antagonist's name on paper and put in a plastic bag of water in your freezer. Put their lawyer's name on paper and anoint it with Bend Over oil, then burn it. In the same manner, place your lawyer's name on paper and anoint it with success oil, and place on your altar for the duration of the case. Finally, put the name of your judge (if you know it) on a piece of paper and stick in a jar of honey to sweeten his or her attitude toward you and your case. All this works best if you are in the right.

Boudica

April 7
Monday

1st ♋

Second Quarter 4:31 am
☽ v/c 2:14 pm

Color of the day: White
Incense of the day: Clary sage

An Invisibility Cloak

Just as in *Harry Potter*, we Witches are able to create our own invisibility cloaks. It is also very quick and simple to do!

Ground and center. Align. Gather in beautiful white light, and cloak it around you. Once the light is all-encompassing, feel and see how your own dense body simply melts away into the white light. Your skin, muscle, flesh, hair, blood, marrow, bone ... all becoming sensuous, soft light.

Seal the spell by chanting:

Cloak of invisibility,

I now decree,

Protect and guard

And shield me.

Gede Parma

April 8

Tuesday

2nd ♋

☽ → ♌ 5:50 am

Color of the day: Scarlet

Incense of the day: Cedar

Spell to Make Peace with Your Sexuality

For this spell, you'll need a cowrie shell, a crystal, a purple candle, and a small vial of Aphrodite or Beltane oil. Set a romantic tone in the room with candles and music. Stand before your altar and tell your chosen deities you are there to make peace with your sexuality. Sprinkle saltwater from your altar vessel over yourself, telling all present that you are cleansing yourself of your old patterns in this realm. Then relax into a deep meditation about your sexuality. Allow yourself to explore without judgment or hurry. Afterward, accept your personal truths by touching both the cowrie and the crystal, acknowledging that they represent your female and male sides, respectively. Seal the truth within them and yourself with the oil, and as the candle burns, say:

I remember who I am.

Leave the cowrie and crystal on your altar, or place them in your medicine bag or pocket, to remind you of this spell and your sacred truths.

Thuri Calafia

 April 9

Wednesday

2nd ♌

Color of the day: Yellow

Incense of the day: Honeysuckle

hone Your Artistic Talent with Athena

The goddess Athena has associations with Wednesday, and many people overlook that, aside from being a great warrior, she also reigns over handicrafts as well as music and the arts. Today's Mercurial energies, along with its connection to Athena, make it a perfect time to work with her to hone any artistic or technical skills you may wish to develop further.

Gather whatever supplies you need to work on your skill, as well as an orange candle and a quartz crystal point to amplify the energy of your spell. Set the candle near your workspace, with the crystal at the base of the candle, crystal pointed toward you. Light the candle and recite the following:

Warrior Athena, strong with might,

Please shine upon me your creative light.

Ancient goddess, resourceful and wise,

Let me see with inspired eyes.

Candle of orange, success, and creativity,

And crystal of quartz to amplify this energy.

So mote it be!

Blake Octavian Blair

NOTES:

April 10
Thursday

2nd ♌

☽ v/c 2:26 am

☽ → ♍ 6:08 pm

Color of the day: Turquoise
Incense of the day: Jasmine

National Library Week

Every library is different—in age, size, shape, and in the numbers of books collected. During National Library Week, set aside some time to visit your local library, and explore a section you never enter or rarely use. If you are already very familiar with your local "book repository," explore one outside of your area. Look to see what types of books on Wicca and earth-based religions they offer. Sit and take in the quiet of unfamiliar surroundings as you research and copy a spell or spells you may never have seen or heard of. Look into the life of Andrew Carnegie, whose philanthropic endeavors over a century ago created many libraries still in use today. Before and after your visit, offer a blessing for literacy.

Emyme

April 11
Friday

2nd ♍

Color of the day: Purple
Incense of the day: Alder

Ask the Oracle

Romans traditionally consulted the oracle at Fortuna's temple on this day. They drew slips of oakwood from a jar, and took the advice printed there to heart.

Today, consult your own oracle. Whether it's a friend who reads tarot cards, a local psychic, or runes that you cast for yourself, readings can offer great insight through symbol and association.

Years ago, I saw a technique in a movie that I often use. Find a copy of your favorite book—literature is recommended. (In the movie it was a Charlotte Brontë novel, I think.) Hold the book in your hands while you formulate your question. Aloud, ask your question of the book, then open it. The answer to your question will appear on the page where you have opened. Allow your mind to stay open and the powers of association to work with the symbols you are given. Within these words lies the wisdom of the oracle.

Dallas Jennifer Cobb

April 12
Saturday

2nd ♍

☽ v/c 1:12 pm

Color of the day: Blue
Incense of the day: Ivy

honor the Goddess Ceres

Today is the first day of the festival of Ceres, the Roman goddess of grains and crops. Ceres represents the fertile earth; she pushes the sprouts from their seeds and offers the promise of an abundant harvest to come. Set your altar with bread, milk, and honey, and a vase of poppies in honor of Ceres. Light a beeswax candle and visualize endless fields of golden grain. Grain symbolized abundance for the Romans; bread and grain were even used to pay soldiers. It was the measure of success. As you meditate on this, you may recite this blessing,

Lady Ceres, bless our seed,

May we never want or need.

Wave your hand across our fields,

Nurture our abundant yields.

Drink a toast to Ceres. Taste the bread, milk, and honey, and leave some as an offering to this goddess of growth and abundance.

Mickie Mueller

April 13

Sunday

2nd ♏

☽ → ♎ 4:33 am

Color of the day: Orange
Incense of the day: Marigold

Palm Sunday

Bless This Food

During any regular ritual, use an edible incense, such as sage or cinnamon—anything that can be used in cooking. Afterward, save the remains of the candle you used for the element of fire, some incense for air, some water (water), and pinch of the salt used for earth.

Assemble these magical ingredients with your cooking ingredients and say:

May the balance of ritual be brought to my home and family as we eat this meal.

(Modify the words for your own intention and living situation.)

Add the incense and say:

By air may we be wise.

Light the candle and touch its flame to your gas burner or outdoor grill. For an electric stove, pass the flame symbolically under the pot. Say:

By fire may we be strong.

Add the water and say:

By water may we be loving.

Add the salt and say:

By earth may we be secure.

Enjoy your meal!

Deborah Lipp

NOTES:

April 14

Monday

2nd ♎

Color of the day: Gray
Incense of the day: Neroli

Takayama Beautification Ritual

On this day, the town of Takayama, Japan, holds a springtime festival featuring flowery floats and summoning a bountiful harvest year. Today's aspects also make this a lovely day to work magic related to beautifying one's life with harmony, balance, and blessings.

Create an altar that prominently features fresh flowers and seasonal fruit. You might also consider adding candles, sweet-smelling incense, and/or a representation of fairies or a love/beauty/luxury goddess of your choice (perhaps Lakshmi, Hathor, or Aphrodite). Sit in front of your altar, close your eyes, and place one hand on your heart and the other hand over it. Take some deep breaths and relax. Then say:

Beauty, I summon you.

Beauty, I welcome you into my body, mind, spirit, and life.

All elements are in harmony.

Luxurious blessings abound.

My smile is sublime because my soul is at peace.

Blossoming sweetness is my perfume,

And I attract all good things.

Tess Whitehurst

Notes:

April 15

Tuesday

2nd ♎

☽ull ☾oon in ♎ 3:42 am

☽ v/c 3:42 am

☽ → ♏ 12:20 pm

Color of the day: Red
Incense of the day: Cinnamon

Passover begins – Lunar Eclipse

Be a Moon Shouter!

The moon is full today at 3:42 am (EST), and we'll also see a total lunar eclipse, visible from Australia, the Americas (including Alaska), the Pacific Islands, and westernmost Africa. At totality, the moon will appear smoky red, a gorgeous subterfuge caused when the limited sunlight passes through the edges of Earth's atmosphere and "scatters," leaving the longest—reddest—wavelengths intact and giving the eclipsed moon its classic rosy color.

As you watch the eclipse, reflect on what this spectacle must have looked like to ancient peoples, who watched the moon turn bloody red and surely imagined disaster was immanent. Many of them imagined the moon was being swallowed by a demon or a mythical animal, and they would should at the moon, cursing it and throwing objects to drive away the invader. Join this ancient tradition as you watch the eclipse. Light a fire or, if that's not possible, a candle or lantern. Dance around the flames, becoming rowdier as you proceed. Shout at the moon, throwing small pieces of dirt, seed heads, pine cones, or other "soft" objects toward the eclipsed satellite, demanding the demons and monsters depart. Shout again, calling back the moon's bright silver face. As the eclipse fades, yell and sing with joy and rejoice in the moon's safe return, feeling the connection you've forged with the ancients. Finish with cakes and ale.

Susan Pesznecker

NOTES:

April 16
Wednesday

3rd ♏

Color of the day: White
Incense of the day: Marjoram

A Pansy Love Spell

Pansies, one of the flowers of spring, are an excellent ingredient to use in love spells because they attract love.

For this spell, you'll need two pink candles, a small bowl of water, and at least one pink or rose-colored pansy plant. Light the candles. Then pick two flowers from the pansy plant, and let them float in the bowl of water until they touch. Slowly move the candles together as you say:

Fate be wise, fate be kind.

Bring me the one, who should be mine.

Let the candles burn down. Plant the pansy in your garden and lavish it with attention. Your love life will grow as the pansy flourishes.

James Kambos

 ## April 17
Thursday

3rd ♏

☽ v/c 3:09 am

☽ → ♐ 5:44 pm

Color of the day: Crimson
Incense of the day: Apricot

Laugh It Up

We know stress in one area of life has a way of creeping into other areas as well. Sometimes we need to sit back and laugh it off.

This spell will get you laughing and relieve stress as well. All you need is someplace where you can yell—preferably a place where you can yell without the neighbors hearing you. Though they may get a laugh out of it, they may also think you're nuts!

The words to this spell are simple. Think of the most goofball things you can possible think of and yell them. They don't have to make sense; in fact, the less sense they make, the better. Just yell silly sounds, and if you want, actually imagine your neighbors overhearing you. It's hard to take yourself seriously when doing this, and it's even more fun if you can get a friend to join in.

Kerri Connor

April 18

Friday

3rd ♐

Color of the day: Coral
Incense of the day: Vanilla

Good Friday

Connect with Your Kids

This is a practical tip to improve communication with your kids, but the results could be absolutely magical. Take them for a drive. I have had some of the best conversations ever with my daughters while it's just us in the car. It works best if it's just one of them with me, because they aren't competing for my attention, but sometimes I've had great discussions with them both present.

Pick a child up from school for a little one-on-one time. Make it just the two of you as they head to a doctor or dental appointment. Have them to run an errand or go shopping with you. Ask how their day went, or how lunch was. Ask after a friend of theirs that you know about. The trick is to open the door for them to talk, so don't force it or make it seem like an inquisition.

Laurel Reufner

 April 19

Saturday

3rd ♐

☽ v/c 9:17 pm
☽ → ♑ 9:28 pm
☉ → ♉ 11:56 pm

Color of the day: Brown
Incense of the day: Sage

Break Down the Wall

What stops you in life? What thoughts and beliefs get in the way of your success or happiness? What do you say to yourself that holds you back? What are your fears?

You will need a gold candle, quick-drying clay, a hammer, and newsprint or rags to protect your work surface or altar.

Light the candle. Meditate on something that holds you back, while forming a small brick out of clay. Name the brick: "This is fear" or "This is low self-esteem."

Meditate on the next barrier while you make the next brick.

Build a wall of bricks, naming each one as a barrier. When the wall is finished, allow it to dry.

When the wall is dry and hard, dance, sing, or drum to generate joyful energy. Then SMASH the wall with the hammer. Scream, laugh, or sing:

I am free! My wall is gone!

Deborah Lipp

April 20
Sunday

3rd ♑

Color of the day: Amber
Incense of the day: Almond

Easter

A Great Mother Omelet

Named after Eostre, the great mother goddess of the Northern European Saxons, and Eostra, or Ostara, the Teutonic goddess of fertility, Easter is the day to celebrate the resurrection of the earth's fertility.

The first Sunday following the full moon after the spring equinox is a time to honor the great mother goddess. Make a "great mother" omelet using common Easter symbols of resurrection from the mammal, fowl, and plant worlds. Assemble some aged cheese, cream, eggs, and spinach. Melt a little butter in a skillet. Scramble two eggs and two tablespoons of cream, with a pinch of salt and pepper. Pour into the pan. Add a huge handful of spinach, and aged cheese to taste. As the eggs cook, flip one side up and over the other, sealing the spinach in the middle. Cover and simmer for two minutes, and make toast. Today, eat reverentially, and know the world is reborn.

Dallas Jennifer Cobb

April 21
Monday

3rd ♑

☽ v/c 7:21 pm

Color of the day: Silver
Incense of the day: Rosemary

A Polarity Spell

Balance is what keeps the world in order. Light and dark, day and night, hot and cold, wet and dry, male and female, positive and negative. With too much of any one thing and not enough of the other, everything collapses and dies. It is the cycle between extremes that makes life possible. It makes magic possible, too, as we move energy from one place to another.

For this spell, you need a magnet with two distinct ends, ideally a rod or a horseshoe. Suspend the magnet from a string and charge it with these words:

Sun and shadow,

Day and night,

Balance all with

Magic's might.

What is low will

Rise up high;

Overflow will

Pass on by.

Whenever you need more of a given energy, tap the positive end of the magnet to raise it. When you need to release something, tap the negative end to do that.

Elizabeth Barrette

 April 22

Tuesday

3rd ♑

☽ → ♒ 12:18 am

Fourth Quarter 3:52 am

Color of the day: White
Incense of the day: Ylang-ylang

Earth Day – Passover ends

Celebrate the Earth

On Earth Day, the possibilities for honoring thy mother are many. Partake in your community's spring cleanup, or fashion a decoration made from recycled materials for your yard or garden. Research organic gardening, eating, and composting. Determine to make one change, no matter how small, in your consumption and/or disposal of precious resources. At the very least, offer up a small blessing or spell for the renewal of the earth.

May there be good health and healing for this Earth,

May there be Beauty above me,

May there be Beauty below me,

May there be Beauty in me,

May there be Beauty all around me.

I ask that this world be filled with Peace, Love, and Beauty.

(Earth Healing Ceremony, Medicine Grizzly Bear, Spokane, WA, 1990.)

Emyme

April 23
Wednesday

4th ♒

☽ v/c 12:10 pm

Color of the day: Topaz
Incense of the day: Bay laurel

Divination

Wednesday is considered the day of the week for you to get in touch with your divination side. Weekly practice with your divination tool of choice is recommended.

My preferred method is tarot, but runes, stones, tea leaves, or palmistry are always good choices. So are dreams, be they sleeping dreams or meditation (waking) dreams.

A diary is a must to keep at hand, to write down your divination, its results, its perceived meanings, your emotional responses, or those little "pop-up" clues that come to you as you do your divination work. Later you can reread and add to the material—thoughts that occur to you after the fact, maybe something that struck you as strange or important, or something you forgot. You can also research what you found and see what other meanings may be there.

Boudica

April 24
Thursday

4th ♒

☽ → ♓ 2:55 am

Color of the day: White
Incense of the day: Clove

Charm for Keeping Away Unwanted Sexual Advances

Cut two circles of white cotton cloth (approximately 3–4 inches in diameter), and draw a pentagram on one before sewing them together, right sides in, leaving a 2-inch opening in the seam for stuffing the charm. Turn and stuff the charm with equal parts of cinnamon, heather, mugwort, lavender, and echinacea, with a tiny "seed" crystal to amplify and enhance the energies, while chanting:

This is my sacred circle,

Inside it, I am safe.

The blue-white light surrounds me,

And power flows through my veins.

They shine within and through me—

East, south, west, north, all.

The Lord and the Lady protect me from harm,

I reach toward their light when they call.

And this is my sacred circle,

Where positive energy flows.

Bound by their light, it is I who decides

Who enters, who touches, who goes.

Wrap this charm in silk or a human-made fiber (to hold the vibrations in) until it's time to use it.

Thuri Calafia

NOTES:

April 25
Friday

4th ♓

☽ v/c 4:03 pm

Color of the day: Rose
Incense of the day: Thyme

Spell to Connect with Air Faeries

On a cloudy day, when you have free time, go to a place outside where you can lay in the grass and cloud watch. When you are relaxed and feel ready, chant this spell to call out to the air faeries so that they may show themselves through the clouds:

Magical sylph, living air.

Send to me a signal so fair.

Shape the clouds in images clear,

That into your realm I may peer.

Pay close attention to the shapes the clouds take after you chant the spell. It is a good idea to bring a notebook to journal your thoughts after you are finished. Repeat this as often as desired, and your relationship to the air faeries will grow.

Michael Furie

April 26

Saturday

4th ♓
☽ → ♈ 6:01 am

Color of the day: Black
Incense of the day: Magnolia

To Ignite the Sight

To ignite and empower your innate Sight, here is a spell for psychic enhancement.

Sitting before your altar or your divinatory medium, ground, center, and align. Close your eyes and allow the Inner Eye to open wide. Behold and perceive it gazing out into the Abyss. Become aware of your body's response to this opening. Sink into those responses and record them in your subconscious to arise at any time.

Take smoky quartz or rainbow obsidian and channel these feelings into the stone as well, praying to the Spirit of the Stone that it may aid you in your work.

Now, whenever you require the wide-opened Eye, you may call up those feelings in your body by holding the stone and praying to your ally.

Gede Parma

April 27

Sunday

4th ♈
☽ v/c 7:02 am

Color of the day: Yellow
Incense of the day: Eucalyptus

This Cat has Claws

Claws are symbolically protective, and are made even more so by the magical application of magnetic nail polish. It comes in many colors, but it's the iron filings in it that make it magnetic. You can use it for protection to ward off psychic attack or negativity. Pick up a bottle of magnetic nail polish, drop a small quartz crystal chip into the bottle, and shake well. Use a base coat, and after it dries, paint the magnetic polish on one fingernail and immediately, before it dries, hold the design magnet over the nail while you repeat this incantation:

Magnetic power I now draw,

Impart your power to my claw.

Shield of iron I now bind,

This cat has claws, protection is mine.

Repeat to all your nails. Apply a topcoat. Please don't scratch anyone, but rest easy knowing you have ten tiny psychic shields in place to protect you from negativity.

Mickie Mueller

April 28
Monday

4th ♈︎

☽ → ♉︎ 10:23 am

Color of the day: Ivory
Incense of the day: Narcissus

Performance for Flora

Today is the first day of the festival of Floralia, which is a celebration of Flora, Roman goddess of spring, flowers, and vegetation. To celebrate, ancient Romans wore garlands of flowers and their most festive attire, and even decked their livestock and animals in flowers of the season. Drinking, merrymaking, games, and performances were held in honor of the goddess and the season.

Today, wear colorful attire in honor of the occasion. Find an opportunity to give an offering of a devotional performance in nature in honor of Flora and the spring vegetation in anyway you feel moved. You could quietly read a poem aloud in a special private spot in nature, you could go into your yard and drum among the trees, or you could have a family procession around the perimeter of your home chanting, drumming, and signing. Whether your celebration is high-profile or low-key, focus on your gratitude for the season and its deities!

Blake Octavian Blair

April 29
Tuesday

4th ♉︎

New Moon in ♉︎ 2:14 am

Color of the day: Gray
Incense of the day: Basil

Solar Eclipse

Rest and Restore

The new moon is a time to rest, recuperate, and restore balance and energy to our lives. So often we are on "go, go, go." We have to stop and remind ourselves to take a break. We have to let our minds and bodies slow down, and possibly even heal. Use the darkness of the new moon to give yourself a much-needed time-out. If you can, stand outside in the dark, or even just in a window looking out toward the dark night sky, and say:

Rest and restore,

Moon of lore,

Allow me time to mend.

Time to recharge,

Balance my soul,

My heart and mind transcend.

Repeat this chant three times and then settle in for a good night's sleep. Sprinkle a few drops of lavender or jasmine oil on your pillow to help your body fully relax and restore itself.

Kerri Connor

April 30
Wednesday

1st ♉

☽ v/c 11:53 am

☽ → ♊ 4:56 pm

Color of the day: White
Incense of the day: Lavender

Walpurgis Transmutation

It's May Eve, or Walpurgis, traditionally celebrated with bonfires to help fuel and clear the way for all the fresh, growing, birthing energy of May. So go through your home and yard and collect all the dry brush, both literal and figurative. In your yard, this might mean deadheading flowers and pinching off dead branches. In your home, look for things like old papers, trash, and clothes that you no longer wear.

At nightfall, consider burning whatever can be safely burned (such as paper and wood) in your fire pit or fireplace. As it burns, play some victorious, high-spirited music and dance! Feel yourself transforming all that was dead and stuck into brightness, light, and energy. At some point, once or repeatedly, say:

What was old is now new,

What was sleeping is now awake,

What was dark is now alight!

The next day, donate any nonburnable items to charity or otherwise release them.

Tess Whitehurst

Notes:

May

For Witches and Pagans, May marks the "height" of the year, as we see with the Beltane sabbat. This Celtic holiday is the precise opposite of Samhain (Halloween) on the Wiccan Wheel of the Year. While the beginning of November marks a descent into darkness, the beginning of May marks an ascent into light. This is a month of fertility and frivolity, sensuality and human connection, making it a good idea to reflect on sex and sexuality. What is your relationship with sex? Do you overuse or neglect your sexuality? What is your view on orientation? What are your sexual imprints from childhood? Meditating on and studying both sex and sexuality in a cross-cultural context can help you develop a more realistic, balanced, and healthy understanding of this human force of pleasure and reproduction. All too often people choose to ignore or shut off their sexuality or overindulge in their urges. Certainly, either side of the equation is imbalanced. This month is bright, illuminating, celebratory, and sexual. We all have the option and opportunity to positively embrace our relationship with sexuality, and May is the ideal time for it!

Raven Digitalis

May 1
Thursday

1st ♍ ♊

☽ v/c 7:32 pm

Color of the day: Green
Incense of the day: Jasmine

Beltane

Creative Fire Burning

A fire festival celebrating sexuality and fertility, Beltane was traditionally when young women slept outdoors. Tonight, wherever you sleep, create darkness and ritually cultivate the wild within. Then ignite a small light, and sow creative brilliance in your fertile soil. Unite male and female—active/receptive, form/creativity, light/dark—to produce creative "babies." From the dark recesses of sexuality, spirituality, and ancient wisdom grow our greatest masterpieces.

Gather a candle, matches, drinking water, paper, and pen. Arrange your tools, then sit in darkness. Envision the forest glade. Create sacred space. Invoke fairies and forest folk for protection. Light the candle:

The fires of Bel burn within,
True passion burns bright.

Sip water:

I water fertile creativity, blessing and good fortune tonight.

Ask yourself:

What do I want to birth/create?

Use pen and paper and write without stopping, without thinking. Write until your creative idea, your "baby," comes to light.

Dallas Jennifer Cobb

NOTES:

May 2
Friday

1st ♊

Color of the day: Pink
Incense of the day: Mint

Decorate with Feeling Spell

It's spring, and the Sun is in Taurus. This is a good time to decorate your home. But decorate with feeling. What do I mean by that? It's been proven that colors emit energy and that we can "feel" colors. This spell will help you increase your visualization techniques and psychic awareness and heighten your intuition.

You can use this spell to help you magically select your paint colors. To begin, go to a paint store and look at all the colors that appeal to you. Take home swatches of those colors. Next, cut the swatches apart so all the colors are separated into neat strips or squares. Put the color samples into a brown paper bag or a box. Shake well, then reach in and without looking, touch the samples. Pull out those that feel right to you. Then look at your selections. You'll be surprised.

James Kambos

May 3
Saturday

1st ♊

☽ → ♋ 2:13 am

Color of the day: Brown
Incense of the day: Pine

Protecting Freedom

This is World Press Freedom Day. It's all about freedom of speech and freedom of expression in all its forms. To Pagans, it touches our right to talk and write about our religion. In some places, these rights are protected, and Pagans are more visible. In other places these rights are not protected, and Pagans are often silenced or even hunted. Freedom is knowledge; knowledge is power.

This spell is about protecting that freedom and its power. As a focus, you'll need a banned book, preferably a Pagan one. Charge it with this invocation:

The magic flies down hidden ways

And sleeps in secret words,

Then frees its voice in brighter days

To soar like wild birds.

Whenever you find an article about freedom of speech, tuck it between the pages and repeat the incantation in support of that freedom. What we will, will be.

Elizabeth Barrette

May 4
Sunday

1st ♋

Color of the day: Orange
Incense of the day: Heliotrope

Blessing with Air: Reading the Wind

Walk in the wind and learn the breezes as they rise and fall: their directions, their temperatures, their scents. Read the weather changes that follow each breeze. Listen to the sound the wind makes as it moves through the trees, rustles leaves, or whips flags. Blow dandelion seed tufts or soap bubbles into the air. Fly a kite or make a paper airplane—either one can be inscribed with runes or infused with spells to carry your magicks into the sky. Lie on your back on the ground and watch the clouds, studying how they form and move and what sorts of weather they portend. Scry the clouds, reading their symbols and patterns. Outside, hang banners and wind chimes and pinwheels. Inside, fill vases with dried flowers and feathers. Wear scarves of gossamer silk that sift and twirl with the breeze. Breathe deeply, feeling the blessings of air surround you!

Susan Pesznecker

May 5
Monday

1st ♋

☽ v/c 4:46 am
☽ → ♌ 1:55 pm

Color of the day: Lavender
Incense of the day: Rosemary

Cinco de Mayo

Housework Meditation

Let's face it: living with others can get tense at times, and you can't always walk out the door until things cool off. The next time everyone starts to get on your last nerve, take a deep breath and take a housework break. Many people admit that they find some forms of housework to be meditative, and for good reason. The semi-mindless repetitive actions can be very soothing.

So the next time the young kids are squabbling, the spouse is being grouchy, the parents don't understand, or the housemates are merely being, well, themselves, go fold some laundry or wash the dishes. Let the repetition give your mind time to wander off and relax. You should be able to return to the fray refreshed and recharged.

Laurel Reufner

May 6

Tuesday

1st ♐ ♌

☽ Second Quarter 11:15 pm

Color of the day: Scarlet
Incense of the day: Bayberry

Spell to Find Your Patron God

Many who come to the Pagan path don't wish to work with male deities for a while, but once you feel it's time, it can be helpful to use guided meditation to find and connect with your personal patron god. *Patron* is from the Old French, meaning "father." You can find yours by simply casting a circle, inviting the quarters, and asking him to reveal himself to you. Bring an offering of frankincense and fresh herbs, and lay these on your altar as a thank-you gift. Deepen into meditation.

In your meditation, look to the edge where shadow meets light in a forest or sacred grove. Open yourself to his energies, and tell him, in your own words, that you're ready to meet him, to receive his truths and guidance. Allow yourself to see him however he presents himself to you, whether dark or light, and be blessed with his protection and gentle strength.

Thuri Calafia

May 7

Wednesday

2nd ♌

☽ v/c 6:50 am

Color of the day: Brown
Incense of the day: Honeysuckle

Garden Talk

Today is a day for communication, so let's get talking—to your plants. Indoors or outside, plants, seedlings, sprouts, and seeds are waiting to burst forth. This spell will help them all grow with abundance. Recite this spell to your plants as you water them, or any other time they seem to need a pick-me-up:

Earth, air, water, sun,

Combine together,

Grow into one.

Roots grow deep,

Leaves grow long,

Make this plant

Good and strong.

Repeat this spell several times. You can turn it into a song and sing it to your plants as well.

Kerri Connor

May 8

Thursday

2nd ♌

☽ → ♍ 2:24 am

Color of the day: White
Incense of the day: Balsam

White Lotus Meditation

Helena Blavatsky, founder of the Theosophical Society, died on this date in 1891. Since then, it has been known to Theosophists as White Lotus Day, a day to meditate on the spiritual symbolism of the lotus.

To participate in this custom, and to reap its benefits, sit comfortably with your spine straight. Relax your body and breathe naturally as you passively observe your breath moving in and out. When you feel ready, consider a lotus. Think about how it receives its perfect nourishment from the murky depths of a pond or a lake, and how it reaches up toward the light, emerges through the water's surface, and rests there peacefully as a pure, voluptuous bloom. Now, hold the image of the blossom in your mind as you breathe in and out, allowing its peaceful vibration to permeate your awareness. Finally, mentally place this blossom at your heart center, and open your eyes.

Tess Whitehurst

May 9

Friday

2nd ♍

☽ v/c 6:08 pm

Color of the day: Coral
Incense of the day: Rose

Children's Book Week

As part of Children's Book Week, look into the schedule of activities for children at your local library. If this is not an option for you, ask at the library about their wants and needs in the children's section. Every library has a list of books they wish for or plan to purchase. Do you have a favorite book from your childhood that is still in print? Or consider age-appropriate books on the history of Stonehenge, how-to gardening, or the care of pets—topics in line with a Wiccan lifestyle. You may also look into purchasing and donating a children's book in honor or in memory of a loved one. The staff will be happy to assist you in completing any forms.

Emyme

May 10
Saturday

2nd ♏

☽ → ♎ 1:19 pm

Color of the day: Black
Incense of the day: Patchouli

To Silence Online Gossip

The best way to stop gossip is not to start it. However, posting on social networks has brought about the endless cycle of starting a rumor. Even if we find out it's not true, there are so many more people who will click and forward without so much as thinking.

Do your part to end online gossip by checking before you click "share." Morgan Freeman has been declared dead so often that it's become a running joke on the Internet.

Always fully read what you are about to share, check the information for accuracy, and then carefully reflect on what you are about to share. Will it hurt anyone? And will it eventually hurt you?

Remember these words:

Read, check, then consider.

If you share with care,

No remorse will you bear.

Boudica

Notes:

May 11
Sunday

2nd ♎

☽ v/c 8:51 pm

Color of the day: Gold
Incense of the day: Frankincense

Mother's Day

Blessings of the Mother

On Mother's Day, there's so much pressure to love your mother, but that can be complicated. Maybe you never knew your mother, or you've lost her, or she was abusive or cold. Maybe you have more than one mother. Maybe you're a mother yourself.

Write a meditation, blessing yourself for the mother(s) you have or don't have and/or for the mother you are. Begin with the love of the Earth Mother, and simply tell the truth. It might say:

I am loved by the Earth Mother.
I remember my mother with love.

Or it might say:

I am loved by the Earth Mother. I feel that love when I remember neglect.

Or:

I am loved by the Earth Mother. I feel that love when I wonder who my birth mother was.

When you're ready, light a blue candle and recite your meditation. Feel loved.

Deborah Lipp

NOTES:

May 12
Monday

2nd ♎︎

☽ → ♏︎ 9:07 pm

Color of the day: Silver
Incense of the day: Hyssop

healing for Those Who heal Others

Today is the birthday of Florence Nightingale, an English nurse who founded the first secular nursing school and helped pave the way for nursing to become an established profession. Today, in honor of Florence, focus on sending healing to all who have dedicated themselves to helping heal others.

Gather a purple candle, an appropriate candle holder, and a healing oil such as lavender. Hold the candle between your hands, and focus on the intention of sending healing to all those in the medical and healing arts professions. Anoint the candle with the oil and then light the candle and recite the following incantation:

Candle flame, burning bright,
surround those who heal in
healing light. So mote it be!

Visualize a growing, radiant purple healing energy emanating from the candle as it burns. It is important to remember that even healers sometimes need healing.

Blake Octavian Blair

May 13
Tuesday

2nd ♏︎

Color of the day: White
Incense of the day: Cedar

hawthorn Spell for Protection

May 13th is the first day of Huath (hawthorn) month in the Celtic tree calendar used by many modern Pagans and Witches. Hawthorn is a good plant to grow as a hedge, as it is protective for the home. There are taboos against bringing it indoors, so I won't suggest doing so (just in case). An excellent protection for your home is to plant a hawthorn bush in your front yard or to buy some dried hawthorn and tie it up in a red cloth bag and bury it in your front yard. Either way, as you plant say the words:

Ancient hawthorn, faery tree,

Protect my home and family.

Spirit roots, grow deep and strong,

Protect from any who would do wrong.

If you have planted a live plant, take special care of it always. If you have used the dried hawthorn as a charm, replace it every three months.

Michael Furie

May 14

Wednesday

2nd ♏

Full Moon in ♏ 3:16 pm

☽ v/c 3:16 pm

Color of the day: Yellow

Incense of the day: Bay laurel

Spell of the Crescent–Crowned Goddess

In the WildWood Tradition of Witchcraft, our Crescent-Crowned Goddess has taught us that "drawing down the moon" is a spell and not a possessory rite.

Stand outside under the full moon and have a small fire burning in a fireproof container before you. To draw down the moon, ground and center, align, and open your arms to the heavens. Let the silver-white light of her radiance pour into you. As it does, begin to visualize in full detail the outcome of your desires. They will come to pass by the next full moon. Let a buildup of saliva collect in your mouth, and at the peak of power, spit on the fire and seal the spell by saying:

I draw down the moon,

And I ask for this boon!

I sing the song of the Witch,

And I cast this spell into the night!

Gede Parma

May 15

Thursday

3rd ♏

☽ → ♐ 1:44 am

Color of the day: Turquoise

Incense of the day: Carnation

Mercuralia

Today is the ancient Roman festival of Mercuralia, honoring the god Mercury, who ruled over travel, communication, and commerce. On this day, it was traditional to sprinkle one's head, ships, and wares with water from the well at Porta Capena in order to receive Mercury's blessings on one's business.

Even if you don't live in Rome near the Porta Capena, you can still bring Mercury's blessings upon your finances. Make a Mercury business wash by boiling water with three bay leaves (bay laurel). While it boils, trace the astrological symbol for Mercury (☿) over the water to invoke Mercury's blessings. Once it cools, sprinkle a bit on your head and hands. You can also sprinkle it on your business card, check stub, or wallet. If you sell anything online, go to your website and then place three drops on the edge of your computer.

Mickie Mueller

May 16
Friday

3rd ♐

☽ v/c 3:43 am

Color of the day: Purple
Incense of the day: Cypress

Succulent, Sweet Life

Today, the French celebrate the Feast of Saint Honoré, the patron saint of pastry chefs and bakers. Imagine processions of white-clad French bakers carrying Saint Honoré cakes and enormous trays of croissants, pain au levain, brioches, and other treats.

The best kind of celebration is one that reminds us to embrace the sweetness of life, so make today delicious. At lunchtime (when many of us have a break from work), find a bakery, coffee shop, or café with a selection of baked treats. Get a decadent one in a box or bag. Outside, walk smiling through the streets holding your treat reverentially. Smile at people who meet your eye, and say:

Life is sweet.

Sit down (in the sun, if it is out) and carefully unwrap your treat, anticipate it, and bless it in advance. Salivate. As you take that first bite, know how succulently sweet is this life.

Dallas Jennifer Cobb

May 17
Saturday

3rd ♐

☽ → ♑ 4:12 am

Color of the day: Indigo
Incense of the day: Rue

Out of Sorts

Some days it feels like everything is going wrong. Your alarm doesn't wake you up, there is no hot water for your shower, and the coffee maker is on the fritz. You feel like you've been thrown for a loop, or like the world may really be out to get you.

You want to restore some normality and balance to your life. In order to do this, you need a great deal of grounding to get yourself recentered. Find a place where you can sit outside on the ground, up next to a tree if possible. Take a deep breath: as you inhale count to ten, and as you exhale count to ten also. Continue this deep breathing and say to yourself:

Restore my balance,

Restore my strength.

In with the good,

Out with the bad.

Feel your body relaxing and recentering.

Kerri Connor

May 18

Sunday

3rd ♑

Color of the day: Amber
Incense of the day: Juniper

A Celebration of Masculinity

Today is the Feast of Pan (Greece). Take some time today to contemplate all the wonderful qualities and energy patterns we in Pagandom label "male."

Light both a black and a white candle and then, leaving an inch of headspace at the top, make a list of all the things you appreciate about your patron gods, the male authority figures in your life, and male qualities in general. Give the words an active voice, such as *protective* rather than *protection*, *inspiring* rather than *inspiration*, and so forth.

Then, when the list is complete, challenge yourself: write "I am" at the top of the list and contemplate how like your patron gods you really are. Follow up by feasting on "male" foods—whatever that means to you. Be blessed.

Thuri Calafia

 ## May 19

Monday

3rd ♑

☽ v/c 3:02 am

☽ → ♒ 5:58 am

Color of the day: White
Incense of the day: Neroli

Travel Protection Spell

On Monday morning, many people are out the door to travel somewhere. Travel by car is the most common mode of transportation. This includes bus, taxi, or any other type of public land transportation. I like to put a bubble of protection around my vehicle. I concentrate on placing a shield of protection around the car with the intent that I will drive safe; the bubble is to keep out anyone who does not drive in a safe manner. We cannot expect protection if we do not act in a safe manner.

For flying, I have a small bag with some dirt from home, a bird feather, a black stone with a pentacle on it, and a toy compass I got for a quarter. The intent in this spell bag is to fly like a bird, arrive at my destination, and always return home safely.

Boudica

May 20

Tuesday

3rd ♒

☽ v/c 6:21 pm

☉ → ♊ 10:59 pm

Color of the day: Black
Incense of the day: Geranium

Break a Connection

Sometimes relationships seem to hang on in the spiritual realm long after they've run their course in the physical. For instance, an ex-partner's energy might still be hanging around, making it difficult to enter fully into a new, more positive relationship.

But never fear: today is a great day to break this old connection for good. First, get rid of any items that were gifts from, or that remind you of, this person. Then light a bundle of dried white sage, safely dispersing its smoke throughout your home and then around your own body. After extinguishing the sage, sit comfortably, close your eyes, and relax. Enlist Archangel Michael's help as you say:

Archangel Michael, please remove and incinerate any and all cords of attachment to _____, and please place a fiery wall around me, through which no further connection may ever be established, now or in any direction of time. Thank you.

Tess Whitehurst

May 21
Wednesday

3rd ♒

☽ → ♓ 8:18 am

Fourth Quarter 8:59 am

Color of the day: Topaz
Incense of the day: Lavender

Change Your Life Spell

Summer is coming, and the world is green and growing. Take advantage of the seasonal energies now to make changes in your life.

For this spell, you'll need three hard-boiled eggs. Drape your altar with white fabric, and place the eggs before you. Gently press two of the eggs together until the shells crack, then set them aside. The cracking of the shells represents a new beginning. The eggs inside the shells symbolize the Life Spirit waiting to come forth. Crack and peel the third egg to represent the shedding of your old ways. Then eat the egg as you think of what change you want to make. The white of the egg symbolizes all the possibilities before you; the yolk is the Sun, guiding you on your way. Use the other eggs in a recipe, and think of this spell as you prepare it.

James Kambos

May 22
Thursday

4th ♓

Color of the day: Purple
Incense of the day: Nutmeg

You Are What You Eat

Diet plays a major role in maintaining good health. The energy of the earth goes into the plants and animals that become our food, and eventually part of our bodies. Unfortunately, much of the food sold today is not very good for people to eat. It comes from plants and animals grown in unwholesome conditions, and often contains artificial additives, which get passed on to people. We can do better.

Today's spell involves eating one meal made from the healthiest ingredients you can find. Shop local and organic if you can. Lay out the meal on nice dishes, and light a white candle. Then say this blessing before you eat:

Earth to grain, grain to bread,

Bread to body, body to soul—

Good food sustains good health

Through the infinite cycles of life.

Elizabeth Barrette

May 23
Friday

4 ♄ ♓

☽ v/c 2:25 am

☽ → ♈ 12:01 pm

Color of the day: Rose
Incense of the day: Yarrow

Cold Iron to Repel a Curse

The day I was officially cursed was the day I knew I'd arrived as a grown-up Pagan. The curse arose from misplaced anger over an event I had no part in. Nonetheless, I was the target of the curser's wrath and the full-on recipient of said curse, and I was concerned about suffering any ill effects as a result.

My thoughts went immediately to cold iron, a substance known to repel evil, curses, hexes, and malicious magickal critters. The best piece of iron for this is a horseshoe: held or fixed with the points up, U-style, it traps and holds negative or dangerous energies, which is probably why we associate it with good luck. To ward off dark magicks, walk your bounds—around house and property—three times while carrying the horseshoe, then mount it over or close to your home's threshold. You'll be well protected.

Susan Pesznecker

May 24
Saturday

4 ♄ ♈

Color of the day: Gray
Incense of the day: Ivy

Thanks to the Mothers

This day in history was sacred to the Mothers, three goddesses worshipped in Celtic lands for bringing abundance and a good harvest, though we give this day no credit for the actual "Mother's Day" holiday.

Use this day to be thankful for the abundance already in your life. We often think we need more, more, more, and forget to be happy about what we already do have. Take some time to really think about the abundance you have. Do you have a home? A car? Plenty of clothes to keep you warm? You most likely have all of that and a whole lot more. Remind yourself that not everyone does. Thank the Mothers who have brought plenty of abundance into your life so far. You may also want to spend some time thinking about what you can do to help others who might not have nearly as much as you do.

Kerri Connor

May 25
Sunday

4th ♈
☽ v/c 11:58 am
☽ → ♉ 5:28 pm

Color of the day: Yellow
Incense of the day: Hyacinth

Melt Away Ill health

Sometimes you want to give a little extra help to someone dear who's facing a difficult time with their health, be it cancer or some other chronic condition. It's natural to want to help the people we care about.

Remember to visualize the illness leaving the healing recipient's body, leaving it healthy and whole. In your mind's eye, see them standing there whole and strong. Write the name of the affliction on a small slip of paper. On the other side, write the person's name. Fill a paper cup, or empty yogurt container, half full of water. Add the slip of paper to the cup and place in the refrigerator until frozen. The following afternoon, place the "diseased" ice cube somewhere outside where the melting water can run away. In your mind, visualize your loved one's illness melting away with it.

Laurel Reufner

May 26
Monday

4th ♉

Color of the day: Gray
Incense of the day: Lily

Memorial Day (observed)

Sacrifice and Freedom

On Memorial Day, we in the United States honor those who have sacrificed their lives for our freedom.

What are you willing to sacrifice for your freedom?

Find a quiet, private place out of doors, near natural water (a stream, pond, or lake). Spend some time gathering pebbles and thinking about sacrifice. What will you give up? What will freedom be like once you have sacrificed?

Sit by the water with the pebbles in your lap. Notice how they weigh you down.

Pick up a pebble and say, "I sacrifice X," naming the first thing you are willing to give up. Drop the pebble in the water. Enjoy the beautiful sound it makes.

Do this with each pebble until your lap is empty.

Thank the body of water for accepting your sacrifice. When you stand up, notice the feeling of freedom.

Deborah Lipp

May 27
Tuesday

4th ♉

☽ v/c 5:10 am

Color of the day: Black
Incense of the day: Ginger

Conflict Resolution with Mars

Mars, Roman god of war, has great influence over this day. At one time or another, we all find ourselves in conflicts to which we truly wish to find a peaceful resolution.

Write a letter to Mars in red ink (a color associated with Mars) stating your perspective, your understanding of the perspectives of others involved, and your desire to work toward a resolution that is for the highest good of all. Then set the letter aflame in a fireproof cauldron or dish. Visualize the path to a resolution manifesting as the paper burns and turns to smoke. Stay with the cauldron or dish until the paper has completely burned out. Keep your eyes open as possible paths to resolution present themselves to you.

Blake Octavian Blair

May 28
Wednesday

4th ♉

☽ → ♊ 12:47 am

New Moon in ♊ 2:40 pm

Color of the day: Brown
Incense of the day: Bay laurel

hurricane Prep Week

Today falls during Hurricane Preparation Week, reminding us that regardless of where we live and what natural disasters may befall our geographical area, being ready for the unexpected is wise.

Create a "disaster" spell kit. In addition to the usual provisions for daily living, precious items you cannot replace, and pertinent legal documents, be sure to pack a votive cup with a fireproof lid, a votive candle, waterproof matches, and a lighter. Include one or two battery-operated tealights and extra batteries; you may be sheltered in a place where open flame is banned. Small containers of salt and cinnamon (for cleansing and power) will suffice for any spell. Add whatever spices and herbs are important to you. I choose vervain for its general properties, and lavender for its calming effects. Tuck in a small, unobtrusive altar cloth, a pen, and a small notebook.

You now have a simple spell kit that will fit into a plastic, airtight freezer bag. None of these items will

cause a stir should you be forced into a shelter where you cannot share your chosen belief system.

Emyme

NOTES:

May 29
Thursday

1st ♊

☽ v/c 5:59 am

Color of the day: Crimson
Incense of the day: Myrrh

Spell for the Protection of Loved Ones

When you are worried about one or more loved ones, be they far from home or in the next room, you can use this spell to keep them safe through the night. To cast it, either gaze up at the stars (outside or through a window) or close your eyes and visualize the starry night sky and think of the sky and stars as the cloak of the Goddess. When you are ready, chant these words:

Circle of stars, shining bright,

Grant my wish on this night.

Shine down upon those I love,

Protection magic, sent from above.

Keep them safe and well and warm,

Free from danger, fear, and harm.

Take a deep breath, and as you exhale, "breathe out" the power and say:

For the good of all and blessed be.

Michael Furie

May 30
Friday

1st ♊

☽ → ♋ 10:13 am

Color of the day: White
Incense of the day: Violet

Courageous heart

Life gives us challenges, and sometimes we have to be very strong to overcome the difficulties tossed in our path while still remaining true to our own heart. We can strengthen our heart to help us face whatever life hands us. Light a red candle carved with a heart with rays and your favorite symbols for strength. Surround the candle with any of the following: bloodstone, carnelian, aspen leaves, cinnamon, or thyme. Light the candle and hold the index and second fingers of your right hand on your heart chakra. Repeat the following nine times while you focus on the flame:

My heart is strong, brave, and true,

Full of spirit in all that I do.

Allow the candle to burn down. Whenever you need to bolster your heart, place your two fingers on your heart chakra, and it will create a trigger to empower you.

Mickie Mueller

May 31
Saturday

1st ♋

Color of the day: Blue
Incense of the day: Sage

To Blow Away
Unwanted Attention

If you are currently the recipient of unwanted attention, employ this spell to send it away on the shifting wind.

Hold a black feather in your hand. If you know which bird it came from, all the better. Ground, center, and align. Call the spirit of the bird through its feather and call upon the winds. If you have called properly, the winds will come, and the air will shift noticeably.

Focus on the black feather, and ask the spirit of this bird to "fly away" the unwanted attention far away from you.

When the wind is at its height, let go of the feather, let the wind take it, and turn and walk away. Do not look back.

Gede Parma

June

The Roman poet Ovid provides two etymologies for June's name in his poem "The Fasti." The first is that the month is named after the Roman goddess Juno, wife of Jupiter and the patroness of weddings and marriage. That's a nice tie-in, because June is known as the month for weddings. The second is that the name comes from the Latin word *iuniores*, meaning "younger ones," as opposed to *maiores*, meaning "elders," for which May is named. The birthstone is the pearl, or sometimes alexandrite or moonstone. The flower associated with the month is the rose, and roses tend to be abundant and blooming in June in the Northern Hemisphere. The summer solstice, usually on June 21 or 22, is also referred to as Midsummer. In the Northern Hemisphere, the beginning of the meteorological summer is June 1; in the Southern Hemisphere, June 1 is the beginning of the meteorological winter.

Magenta

June 1
Sunday

1st ♋

☽ v/c 2:32 am

☽ → ♌ 9:43 pm

Color of the day: Gold
Incense of the day: Juniper

From Norma Jean to Marilyn

Today is Marilyn Monroe's birthday. This spell is a "glamour" that transforms you from Norma Jean to Marilyn; it gives you a mystique of attraction that transcends mere beauty.

Acquire some rose water, a red rose, a red candle, and a glittery powder (such as a loose eyeshadow or body glitter).

Light the candle and center yourself. Inhale the scent of the rose and think about romance, glamour, and mystique.

Place your hand over the glitter container, pouring energy into it, and say:

Shimmer, sheen, and shine. You are attracted without knowing why!

Add a pinch of glitter to the rose water, saying:

Allure, allure, my heart is pure.

Add a petal from the rose, saying:

Drink of my mystery.

Place the rose water on your pulse points.

Whenever you wish to wear your glamour, renew the rose water on your pulse points.

Deborah Lipp

NOTES:

June 2
Monday

1st ♌

Color of the day: Ivory
Incense of the day: Narcissus

Organize Your Wedding Spell

If you're planning your wedding, you know what a big job it is. After running a formal wear business for years, I know what a chore it can be, so I developed this spell to help your wedding planning run smoothly.

On one sheet of paper, write your to-do list. Include everything: order flowers, find a photographer, etc. On a second sheet of paper, write a list affirming how and when you'll accomplish each task. Lay each list on your altar—the to-do list on the left, and the affirmation list on the right. In the center of your altar, place a pink pillar candle. Each night, light the candle, review each list, and check off completed jobs. When done each night, move the lists closer together. You'll begin to feel in control of the situation as everything comes together—it always does. Blessed be!

James Kambos

June 3
Tuesday

1st ♌

☽ v/c 10:42 am

Color of the day: Maroon
Incense of the day: Cinnamon

Reveal Yourself

Early in June, I open the creaky attic doors and pull out summer clothes. With growing kids, it's a time to release and recycle things that no longer fit. For adults, it's a time to reunite with old favorites, and a time to let go of things that don't fit in other ways.

The physical act of seasonal change-over reminds us to do an emotional, spiritual, and psychic change-over, too. It's time to let go of protective layers and reveal yourself. Do a quick go-through of your summer clothes, asking: *Is this perfect?* Any item that is in poor repair, doesn't fit, is never worn, is unflattering, or holds bad memories needs to go. Put these in a bag, placing them outside the front door. Later, send them along to a new, more appreciative home by donating them to a local charity or secondhand shop. Bless the clothes that remain, and whenever you wear them, remember what you let go of, and what you choose to reveal: *I reveal the true me.*

Dallas Jennifer Cobb

June 4
Wednesday

1st ♌

☽ → ♍ 10:20 am

Color of the day: Yellow
Incense of the day: Marjoram

Celebration of Abundance and Gratitude

As the year waxes, as the moon waxes, so abundance waxes and takes form in my life .... For this spell, take a green taper and carve it with all the symbols of what's coming to fruition in your life, as well as those things you most wish to manifest. Dress it with oil, chanting the above. When energy has been sufficiently raised, shoot it into the candle with the words:

Abundance is mine!
So mote it be.

Next, think about all the things you're grateful for in your life, both those things that have already manifested, and those things you most wish would come to pass. Take a rose (or several!) and think only of how grateful you are for each and every blessing. Breathe your blessing of gratitude into the petals of the rose, and then give it away to the Goddess by floating it on living water.

Thuri Calafia

 June 5
Thursday

1st ♍

Second Quarter 4:39 pm

Color of the day: White
Incense of the day: Mulberry

Grow Business

Nothing spells success like a growing business. We do all we can to increase our business to make ourselves successful.

Make sure your product is always the best you offer. Whether it's handmade, recycled, or purchased, always insist it be your best effort. Being fair is the best way to do business. Hermes/Mercury is considered the god of business; ask him for guidance and assistance with your business.

Call upon your personal muse to assist with good marketing strategies. Have a plan and stick to it. Your muse will assist you in designing all your ideas and make them reality.

Finally, know your customers. Be fair, honest, and polite to your customers, but be firm about what your product is worth. Never undersell or underestimate yourself. Your time, money, and efforts should pay off, not pay out. Always ask your gods for patience when dealing with customers.

Boudica

June 6
Friday

2nd ♍

☽ v/c 5:13 am

☽ → ♎ 10:01 pm

Color of the day: Purple
Incense of the day: Orchid

You Really Like Me

In a small jar or tin, place 3 ounces maple syrup, 1 ounce rose water (or 9 rose petals), a 3-inch cinnamon stick (if necessary, break to fit in your jar), 3 apple seeds, and a small piece of chocolate. On a piece of paper, write the following:

> I, (insert your name), am desirable, loving, and passionate. I am deserving of love and passion in return. Let the attitudes of those I meet be sweetened toward me. Bring me love!

Fold the paper toward you. Rotate it and then fold again. Keep rotating and folding until you can't fold it anymore. Set the jar out of the way on a heatproof surface, place a red candle on top, and allow it to burn itself out. The spell is done.

Laurel Reufner

 June 7
Saturday

2nd ♎

Color of the day: Black
Incense of the day: Patchouli

hidden Matters

Unless you are aware of the hidden matters that are happening in your life and around you, you cannot have complete balance in your life. Is someone being nice to your face but working against you behind your back? Too often that may be the case. Use this meditation to help show you what is going on around you that you cannot yet see:

> Unseen to be seen.
>
> Unheard to be heard.
>
> Truth I see.
>
> Truth I hear.
>
> Unseen. Seen.
>
> Unheard. Heard.

Meditate on these words, allowing yourself to go deeper until you are able to catch glimpses of what may be going on out of sight.

Kerri Connor

June 8
Sunday

2nd ♎

☽ v/c 3:47 pm

Color of the day: Orange
Incense of the day: Marigold

Eve of Vestalia Cleaning

Vestalia is the weeklong celebration of the goddess Vesta, often portrayed as a hearth flame. Traditionally, this was the time of the annual cleaning and preparation of the temple of Vesta. If you are in need of a new besom, or broom, now may be a good time to purchase or craft one. Dispose of the old broom by cleansing it with saltwater. Burn it, if that is convenient, or put it with the recycling. Likewise, cleanse and bless your new broom with the spell below. Use the new tool to chase away the cobwebs, both literal and figurative. Clean the entire house, just one room, or your sacred space. After cleaning, be sure to shake your broom outside—no cobwebby brooms back in the closet!

Salt and sage, cleanse this broom,

Bring to it power for me alone.

Vesta, guard my hearth and home,

Your hearth fire bright in every room.

Emyme

June 9
Monday

2nd ♎

☽ → ♏ 6:38 am

Color of the day: Silver
Incense of the day: Lily

Vesta's Favorite Treat

In ancient Rome, today marked the beginning of the festival honoring the goddess of hearth and fire, Vesta. As an offering to her, the priestesses prepared a simple pastry called mola salsa. Here's a way to make it yourself.

Light a red jar candle and place it near the oven. Preheat to 450° F. Mix together 2 cups spelt flour, 1 tablespoon baking powder, ¾ teaspoon salt, 4 tablespoons margarine, and ¾ cup soy milk. Knead, adding flour if necessary. Roll out flat and cut out round pieces with a cup. Arrange on ungreased cookie sheet and bake for 12–15 minutes.

As they bake, direct your palms toward the oven and say:

Vesta, I prepare these pastries in your honor.

Please bless them with your loving nurturance and beneficent light.

Place one or more pastries on your altar as an offering to Vesta, and enjoy/share the rest with a spread of your choice.

Tomorrow, bury the offerings, or feed them to the birds.

Tess Whitehurst

NOTES:

 June 10
Tuesday

2nd ♏

☽ v/c 10:21 pm

Color of the day: Red
Incense of the day: Basil

Enough and Plenty

Abundance means having not just enough to get by, but plenty to share. It's not all about wealth. It's about time, energy, and other resources, too. Everything in nature cycles. Rain falls, runs to the ocean, and evaporates to fall as rain again. The fire that burns a forest makes ash to nourish new seedlings. Nature doesn't ask for its bounty back; it just keeps giving, moving through the cycle.

For this abundance spell, focus on the law of returns, that what you give influences what you receive. Do three nice things today for people who can't pay you back directly. After each one, find a private moment to recite this charm:

Water flows and fire burns.

What I give forth soon returns.

So abundance comes to me.

As I will, so mote it be.

Make sure nobody overhears you; this is one time when the "to be silent" rule applies.

Elizabeth Barrette

June 11
Wednesday

2nd ♏

☽ → ♐ 11:23 am

Color of the day: White
Incense of the day: Lilac

Cheerful Service

Make a plan to give back to your magickal community, whether in person or online. Perhaps you can host a gathering, teach a class, or lead a ritual? You might be able to lend a hand at the local Pagan Pride Day or a similar event. Are you involved in an online community? Start an informational blog, or consider organizing a set of resources or offering your skills in writing or web design.

Whatever you do, remember that service is a gift—a gift of sharing that should come from the heart. It matters not whether you are expert or amateur. In fact, the word *amateur* comes from the Latin *amare*, "to love," and refers to someone who does something purely for the love of it. Before, during, and after your service, repeat this charm:

From the heart,

A service call,

Given now,

To one and all.

Susan Pesznecker

June 12
Thursday

2nd ♐

Color of the day: Green
Incense of the day: Clove

Blessing for Wedding Rings

It is wise to bless the rings you shall wear (hopefully always) as symbols of your marriage bond. Sometimes, we are not fortunate enough to be able to have a full-fledged Pagan handfasting ceremony due to family differences or other reasons. In that case, a simple but heartfelt private blessing said over the rings is a very effective means of giving them proper direction and magical intent. If possible, slip the rings over the end of a wand or hold them in both hands as you send white light into them and say this spell:

Symbol of union worn on the hand,

Golden circles of eternity,

Protect and nurture the love for which you stand,

Blessed you shall ever be.

Keep the rings in a white or pink magic bag until the ceremony to preserve the charge.

Michael Furie

June 13
Friday

2nd ♐

Full Moon in ♐ 12:11 am

☽ v/c 12:11 am

☽ → ♑ 1:04 pm

Color of the day: Pink
Incense of the day: Thyme

Rose Moon Blessing Water

In Colonial America, the full moon in June was known as the Rose Moon because the roses were in full bloom. Now is the perfect time to make some rose full moon water.

Fill a silver, white, or crystal bowl with spring water, and float a white rose or white rose petals in it. Hold the bowl so you can see the full moon reflected in the surface of the water. As you gaze at the moon's reflection in the bowl, feel its power flowing into the water and rose. Then recite the following incantation to charge the water:

Light my path, blessed lamp of the night,

Infuse with your magic, shine with your light.

By light of the moon I awaken the rose,

In the dark of the night the energy flows.

I herby enchant through my power and will,

And ask of the Goddess blessing magic fulfill.

Allow the bowl to sit outside where the moonlight will shine directly on it for as long as you can, but be sure to retrieve it before sunrise. Seal the water in a dark-colored glass bottle and store it for later use. Use white rose full moon water to bless and purify altar tools, or asperge an area or person that needs purifying.

Mickie Mueller

NOTES:

June 14
Saturday

3rd ♑

Color of the day: Blue
Incense of the day: Pine

Flag Day

Positive Patriotism Spell

Today is Flag Day in the United States. It's a waning moon, and Mercury is retrograde, so consider how to eliminate negativity from expressions of patriotism. Often, patriotism can become a jumble of confused feelings, so today, let's do a clearing.

Prepare three candles: red, white, and blue.

Light the red candle and meditate on bravery. Allow bloodshed, violence, and hate to fall away. Let the courage of your patriotism be pride of a gentle spirit.

Light the white candle and meditate on purity. Allow distrust to fall away. Think of those with whom you disagree fiercely, and trust the purity of their motivations.

Light the blue candle and meditate on justice. Allow the desire to restrict others to fall away in the face of freedom. Understand that justice is a higher motivation than vengeance, and allow the feeling of true justice to drive away anger.

Sing your favorite patriotic song.

Deborah Lipp

June 15
Sunday

3rd ♑
☽ v/c 2:35 am
☽ → ♒ 1:27 pm

Color of the day: Yellow
Incense of the day: Almond

Father's Day

Honoring Father Figures

Today is Father's Day, and on this day it is important to recognize all our father figures, not just the biological ones. Many of us have uncles, neighbors, close friends, or even coven Priests whom we consider family of spirit. Oftentimes the parental bond with these father figures is even stronger than with our biological father, for various reasons.

Today, make it a point to reach out to at least one of these nontraditional father figures in your life, and let them know you appreciate their presence in your life. This acknowledgment in itself is a magickal act, for the emotional exchange that takes place in such relationships is an ongoing manifestation of the Divine. If for whatever reason you cannot contact such a person today, light a candle on your altar in honor of and in gratitude to that person.

Blake Octavian Blair

June 16
Monday

3rd ♒

Color of the day: Lavender
Incense of the day: Hyssop

Fairies at Play

As we get closer and closer to Midsummer, the fairies come out to frolic and play more and more. I love the Fey, I really do. However, I also know that in their "play," they tend to enjoy creating a bit of chaos for those who are more human and mortal. This spell is to allow the Fey their fun, but to help keep it from being at your expense:

Fairy children, come and play,

Have your fun this summer day.

My house, my home, myself, you see,

Shall not be the object of your trickery.

I am safe, I am sound,

While your summer fun abounds.

Have your fun, with the play you do,

And I will leave a gift for you.

Make sure you do leave a gift for the Fey after reciting this spell outside. Trinkets, shiny things, cakes, or other treats are always good ideas.

Kerri Connor

June 17
Tuesday

3rd ≈≈

☽ v/c 2:07 pm

☽ → ♓ 2:26 pm

Color of the day: White
Incense of the day: Ylang-ylang

Purple Bottle Peace Spell

Work can be a stressful, tense place, even if you work from home. This spell bottle can be created to send out waves of calming vibrations throughout your workplace.

You will need a small purple bottle, or a clear glass bottle tied with purple ribbon. By the light of purple and pink candles, fill the bottle with a mixture of two parts lavender buds and one part sea salt, adding peaceful energies with each. Top with a small rose quartz that you have charged to be peaceful and calming. Close the bottle with a cork and, if you wish, drip some of the purple candle's wax around the top. Envision your charm bottle sending out waves of calming vibrations. Another option, if you're placing the bottle on a desk in your home office, would be to fit a purple candle in the opening, which you then burn when you feel the need arise. Make sure to set it on a heat-safe surface that won't be ruined if you get candle wax on it.

Laurel Reufner

June 18
Wednesday

3rd ♓

Color of the day: Topaz
Incense of the day: Honeysuckle

Healing the Earth of Committed Ignorance

Ignorance is not the problem. Education solves this bane. It is commitment to ignorance that is a blight on our planet and its interconnected systems of relationships. Here is a spell that will help to heal the earth of this poison.

Go to the most public piece of open Earth you can find. It would be great if this is at lunchtime in a city, when everyone is walking around. Sit down, close your eyes, and meditate. Either have written or painted on your shirt or on a sign: "I am a Child of Earth."

Some people will notice you, and some will ignore you. This meditation out in the open is an offering to Earth and her peoples. It will shift things. Do this as often as you like.

Gede Parma

June 19
Thursday

3rd ♓

Fourth Quarter 2:39 pm

☽ v/c 3:05 pm

☽ → ♈ 5:26 pm

Color of the day: Purple
Incense of the day: Apricot

Tell It to the Bees Spell

It's been believed since ancient times that bees have a mystical connection with humans, and can sense what's going on in our lives. For this reason, when happy or tragic events occurred, it was customary for a member of the household to go outside and "tell it to the bees." If it was sad news, black fabric or quilts were used to cover hives or part of a grassy area to prevent the bees from leaving. Bees are the most important of all insect pollinators, and without them, our earth would suffer. Honor these industrious creatures that want to be part of our lives by chanting this charm outside:

I honor the flowers, I honor the trees,

But in times of grief or happiness,

I will always tell it to the bees.

The next time you have a problem, whisper it to the bees. They want to help.

James Kambos

June 20
Friday

4th ♈

Color of the day: White
Incense of the day: Alder

Feeding the Spirit
by Fasting the Body

Decide in advance how much time you'll take for this spell—whether you wish to fast during the daylight hours only, beginning your Litha celebration at sunset like the ancients did, or for twenty-four hours, beginning your Litha celebration tomorrow.

At the beginning of your fasting time, take a pillar candle in a color that best represents food, nourishment, and health to you, and carve it with symbols that represent these things, as well as personal enlightenment, and dress it with oil. As you light the candle, ponder world hunger, abundance, nutrition, and starvation. Ponder your personal relationship with food and nourishment. If possible, let the candle burn throughout the day, as you continue the contemplations from above, jotting down any emotions or frustrations you have about these issues.

At the end of the fasting period, burn the paper, releasing frustration, anxiety, and compulsion. When you take your first meal, visualize and give gratitude to all the beings who had a hand in feeding you. Eat slowly and mindfully, letting the food fill you with nourishment.

Thuri Calafia

NOTES:

June 21
Saturday

4th ♈

☉ → ♋ 6:51 am

☽ v/c 6:24 pm

☽ → ♉ 11:03 pm

Color of the day: Brown
Incense of the day: Sandalwood

Litha – Summer Solstice

Summer Solstice for the Solitary

A simple ritual for the summer solstice requires a few candles and sparkles—silver and gold—and lots of white lights. Plus something sparkly to drink, like sparkling cider or grape juice or wine, and some sweet cookies.

Silver and gold represent the colors of the sun and the moon; on the summer solstice, the day is the longest and the night is the shortest. Decorate your altar with the candles and white lights.

We are celebrating the magic of the summer. First, go somewhere and watch the sunset. It will be late in the evening, but it is a wonderful way to start a ritual—sunsets are pure magic. By the time you arrive home, it should be dark. Light up all the white lights and candles. Sprinkle sparkles to create your sacred space and sprinkle them on the altar. Have fun sprinkling them everywhere.

If you feel you want to invite your deity, do so. Call upon the magical folk to join your celebration. Offer some drink and cookies to all. Perform a simple magic spell for yourself (for your happiness and prosperity or good health) and then send all the magic folk home. Thank your deity for joining ... and then sit and enjoy the magic of a summer night.

Boudica

NOTES:

 June 22
Sunday

4th ☐

Color of the day: Amber
Incense of the day: Eucalyptus

Rose Magic

Today we commemorate Saint Alban the Martyr, who was carried through rose bushes before being put to death. While that image is disturbing, I like to think that Saint Alban died happy, surrounded by the intoxicating scent of roses.

Many varieties of roses are blooming now, their sweet, succulent smell addictively uplifting. Walk through your neighborhood, looking for a rose bush. Church gardens and civic buildings are great places to look. Choose a small bloom, still bud-like, but mostly open. Grab the stem and feel the thorns prick your fingers. *Life is filled with pain.* Gently snap the bud off the stem, and hold the flower to your nose. Inhale. *Life is filled with pleasure.*

Repeatedly smell the intoxicating scent as you walk home, being careful not to prick your fingers, consciously choosing pleasure over pain. Place the rosebud on your altar, and remember you always have a choice.

Dallas Jennifer Cobb

 June 23
Monday

4th ☐

☽ v/c 9:49 pm

Color of the day: White
Incense of the day: Rosemary

Sustainable Offerings

Most of us magickal folks believe in some sort of magickal polarity in the universe—a give and take that retains balance. An important part of this involves giving offerings, which replace energy and elements used and thank or perhaps appease those entities that assist us.

In this day and age, with our home planet endangered by environmental damage and rising temperatures, it's important that our physical offerings be items and materials that don't harm the environment and may even benefit it. Rather than offering the traditional silver coins to living water, offer shiny agates or quartz crystals. If strewing seed over the ground, ensure that the seeds are native to the area, avoiding introduction of non-native species. Rather than offering cornmeal, which attracts insects and rot, use dried herbs or a handful of compost. If hanging "cloutie" rags in trees, use natural fabrics like cotton, wool, and linen.

Susan Pesznecker

June 24
Tuesday

4th ♉

☽ → ♊ 7:05 am

Color of the day: Scarlet
Incense of the day: Bayberry

International Fairy Day

This is the most fantastical of days! Of course, you have already made an offering to the fey folk at Midsummer/Litha. Today, continue that celebration by gathering early-morning dew on blotting paper, for use in future spells. You may also wish to set aside small portions of every meal to leave for the folk in your garden. If you have been collecting odds and ends in a junk drawer, choose a few fairie-attractive items and hide them in your home. Finally, before you retire for the night, pour a wee portion of honey, wine, or juice in a cleansed eggshell and place in an out-of-the-way spot on your property. Fairies rarely wish to be seen, so simply leave the gifts with all good wishes and gratitude for any protection granted.

Emyme

NOTES:

June 25
Wednesday

4th ♊

Color of the day: White
Incense of the day: Marjoram

An Idea Day

As the moon approaches new, take a moment to brainstorm new ideas and directions. Light a white or yellow candle and a stick of frankincense or cedar incense, get a notebook and pen, and say the following invocation:

Mercury and spirits of air,

I call on you.

Please quicken and sharpen my mind

So that order, harmony, and success may prevail.

May the seeds I plant today

Beautifully fuel all of my tomorrows.

Begin by brainstorming new ideas, such as career goals, projects or habits you'd like to start, or responsibilities you'd like to let go of. Then take some time with each one. Without censoring yourself, write down everything that comes to mind under each heading.

Once you've reached a completion point with each one, refine and hone your plans and resolutions until you feel positive and exuberant about what you've come up with.

Tess Whitehurst

NOTES:

June 26
Thursday

4ħ ♊

☽ v/c 7:56 am

☽ → ♋ 5:05 pm

Color of the day: Turquoise
Incense of the day: Jasmine

Everything in Its Place

An altar is a center of magic, like the hub of a wheel. It creates a physical manifestation of metaphysical forces. Everything important to you has a place on your altar. The basic tools—wand, athame, chalice, and pentacle—represent universal ideals. However, you can also assemble an altar based on your own personal symbolism. This works well for meditation, or spells to influence your own worldview.

Begin with an empty table. Drape it with fabric in your favorite color. Add things that remind you of the elements and deities, such as photos, figurines, etc. Select items that have personal meaning, not standard items. Then charge the altar:

Symbols from the inner world

Turn their faces outward, twirled,

Now together, now apart,

Dance of body, hum of heart.

Altar table, smooth and fine,

Hold the magic that is mine.

Chosen here with thought and care,

In these images you bear.

Elizabeth Barrette

NOTES:

June 27
Friday

4th ♋

New Moon in ♋ 4:08 am

Color of the day: Rose
Incense of the day: Mint

Releasing Fear

Sometimes fear can leave us too panicked to take action. The new moon is the "zero point" where the lunar cycle renews, and using this time to cast out our fear and move forward can be very effective. You need a cup of water, a cauldron, a black candle, a piece of paper, and pen. To begin, write what you fear on the paper and hold it, pouring your fear into it. Light the black candle. Say:

I return to the beginning to begin anew.

Light the paper in the candle's flame and drop it in the cauldron. Say:

Mother Goddess, hear my plea, banish this fear out of me.

Pour the cup of water into the cauldron and say:

Fear is released into the universal waters; the power builds once more.

Snuff out the candle, and when it has cooled, bury the ashes, water, and candle in the earth.

Michael Furie

 # June 28
Saturday

1st ♋

☽ v/c 9:02 pm

Color of the day: Indigo
Incense of the day: Magnolia

Bless Your Barbeque

A barbeque grill is an extension of your hearth, and some consider it a modern-day cauldron. You'll cook many healthy meals there in the coming months, so why not bless it to infuse those meals with magic?

Fire up your grill. Open the vents and get it blazing. Bundle sprigs of fresh rosemary, sage, and basil with some cotton string. Set the herb bundle on the grill above the fire, and close the top of the grill, allowing the smoke from the herbs to fill the grill. Say:

Herbs of power, herbs of art,

I purify and bless this hearth.

This cauldron I do consecrate,

From flame to fuel, lid and grate.

Each meal shall fill with magic and love,

I call down blessings from above.

Allow the herbs to burn completely. Now your grill is a blessed outdoor hearth. Use it to nurture magic all summer long.

Mickie Mueller

June 29
Sunday

1st ♋

☽ → ♌ 4:43 am

Color of the day: Gold
Incense of the day: Frankincense

A Flame for Love, Truth, and Wisdom

In the WildWood Tradition, we keep, witness to, and aim to embody the three gifts of our beloved Goddess—love, truth, and wisdom. They are crowned by beauty and open the way to the Peace of Paradise; to living with, in, from, of, and by grace.

Light three candles in a variety of colors. One will represent love, another truth, and the last, wisdom. Find a truly beautiful candle, and then one by one add the flames of love, truth, and wisdom to this candle of beauty.

Meditate on the Peace of Paradise. Commit to grace. Chant aloud:

In the name of love… in the name of truth… in the name of wisdom… and by the beauty that crowns them all, in the splendour of Spirit, I am opened to the Peace of Paradise. In grace do I live.

Gede Parma

June 30
Monday

1st ♌

Color of the day: Gray
Incense of the day: Neroli

Taking Time for Internal Balance

On this day in 1972, the first leap second was added to the Coordinated Universal Time system. Because Earth's speed of rotation is irregular, leap seconds are periodically added to a day in order to keep in sync with the mean solar day, which affects the length of the days we perceive on Earth. Today is also Monday, the start of the work week for many.

In honor of the start of the week as well as the anniversary of the leap second, be sure to take a few extra moments of your own to ground and center for the start of the week. Listen to relaxing music and drink a cup of herbal tea. Take time out to do a favorite yoga pose, or simply sit still and breathe deeply for a few moments. Ground, center, and find a place of balance. Always remember to take time as needed to recenter and maintain your internal balance.

Blake Octavian Blair

July

July is the hope of April, the lushness of May, and the growth of June all brought to fulfillment. Now, flower beds are splashed with color, garden-fresh produce appears at roadside stands, and the Grain Goddess watches over ripening crops. The mornings are dewy, and there's a sweetness in the air. On July 4, we pause to remember a special July morning years ago in Philadelphia, when statesmen gathered to declare that a young, struggling nation was free and independent. In colonial times the full moon of July was called the Blessing Moon. Independence Day is the main holiday of the month, celebrated with parades and barbecues. It's also a good day to declare magical goals to free ourselves from bad habits and patterns. With the sun in the water sign Cancer, cleansing and fertility magic of all kinds are appropriate. Simply taking a swim will cleanse your body, mind, and spirit. More than anything, July dazzles us. July is an awesome thunderstorm on a hot afternoon. It's a meadow turned white with Queen Anne's lace, and it's firefly nights. July is summer's song being sung. Sweet July—it's the high note of the year.

James Kambos

July 1
Tuesday

1st ♌

☽ v/c 6:00 am

☽ → ♍ 5:24 pm

Color of the day: Black

Incense of the day: Ginger

A July Money Spell

Traditionally, July was known as the "ripening" time. Gardens begin to produce, and crops are beginning to mature. It's a good idea to perform a money spell now so its power will grow with this season of growth. You'll need a gold or orange candle, a citrine stone, a dollar bill, at least two small mirrors, and a vase of flowers such as black-eyed Susans.

Light the candle. Blow on the citrine to empower it with your magical intent, then rub the citrine over the dollar. Place the mirrors so they reflect the candle, the citrine, the dollar, and the flowers. Lay the dollar in front of the candle with the citrine on it. Visualize the mirrors reflecting and expanding your wealth as you say:

Money green and stone of gold,

Bring me wealth to hold.

Wrap the dollar around the citrine, and don't spend it. Let the candle burn, and keep the flowers until they fade.

James Kambos

 # July 2
Wednesday

1st ♍

Color of the day: Topaz

Incense of the day: Lilac

A Traveling We Go

Many people travel this time of year, whether out of town for a summer vacation or across town for a festival or fireworks display. July is generally a time for travel (and gas) prices to increase. This spell will help you get to your destination safely:

Traveling close or traveling far,

By bike, train, plane, or car,

Keep me safe, all passengers too,

As I take this trip, my plea to you.

Keep me safe, keep me sound,

Protect me 'til I reach where bound.

You can chant this spell before you leave and while on your way as well, especially if you run into difficulties such as turbulence or heavy traffic. Just remember that no spell takes the place of paying attention to the situation around you.

Kerri Connor

July 3
Thursday

1st ♍

Color of the day: Crimson
Incense of the day: Carnation

Spiritual Comfort When You Are Sick

It's not always easy to stay healthy. We eat the right foods and exercise, and still we can get sick. It's really bad when we are alone and don't have anyone to get us through this hard time.

If an illness persists for more than three days, see a doctor. Medical assistance is available to all people, and there is no excuse for not seeing a doctor when it is most needed.

Asclepius and his daughters Hygeia (Health), Iaso (Healing), and Panacea (Cure-All) are good to call upon when you are feeling overwhelmed by illness. Read up on them—they are quite the family!

Or call upon your own gods and/or spirituality for help during a rough bout with illness. Having a friend or family member come check up on you regularly helps, too. And, of course, comfort foods are essential. I recommend chicken soup!

Boudica

July 4
Friday

1st ♍

☽ v/c 12:21 am
☽ → ♎ 5:43 am

Color of the day: White
Incense of the day: Alder

Independence Day

Declare Your Independence

This spell will help you more easily extricate yourself from a bad or dead relationship. You will need a black candle, a heatproof container, and a picture of the two of you. If you don't have a suitable picture, draw stick figures and label them with your names.

Tear the picture in two, and place it in front of the lit black candle. Meditate for a moment on the candle's flame, envisioning yourself whole, healthy, and happy. Now pick up the half of the image with your (former) significant other on it, and set it alight in the candle's flame. Allow it to burn itself out in the heatproof container. Allow the candle to burn itself out, or let it burn for a reasonable amount of time. Take the ashes outside and let the wind carry them away. It is done.

Laurel Reufner

July 5
Saturday

1st ♎

☽Second Quarter 7:59 am

Color of the day: Gray
Incense of the day: Rue

Ritual of Freedom

Assert your independence! Take a moment to ponder what independence and freedom really mean to you. Do these words indicate a life unencumbered, with no commitments to anyone for any reason, or do you feel that the ties that bind are also the ties that free? For some folks, having a strong bond to a coven or a family of friends can help them become more independent.

Write a personal declaration of independence for yourself, honoring the connections that are healthy and productive in your life, and acknowledging the connections that no longer serve. Carve a symbol on a tealight or votive candle for each connection you wish to acknowledge in this spell, and tie a string from you to the light. Then, cut the threads of the outmoded connections with total love and respect, and acknowledge that the ones you choose to keep are part of your freedom, too.

Thuri Calafia

July 6
Sunday

2nd ♎

☽ v/c 11:31 am

☽ → ♏ 3:33 pm

Color of the day: Amber
Incense of the day: Hyacinth

happy, happy, happy

In Pamplona, Spain, today is the beginning of Los Sanfermines, a festival honoring Saint Fermin, which climaxes on July 14th. The opening of the fiesta is celebrated with fireworks and the launch of a giant rocket called "el chupinazo." Los Sanfermines is said to be a long festival celebrating happiness, and at the end, the people of Pamplona traditionally sing, "Poor me, poor me, the San Fermin Fiesta has ended."

Let this inspire you to be happy. Write a gratitude list of ten things you are thankful for or blessed by. It doesn't matter if they're large or small, finite or infinite. Write them down. The act of writing a gratitude list and "counting our blessings" can improve our mood and make us feel happier—true magic at work!

Today, whenever you remember, count your blessings, give thanks for all you enjoy, and be happy! No time to sing "poor me."

Dallas Jennifer Cobb

July 7
Monday

2nd ♏

Color of the day: Silver
Incense of the day: Clary sage

Scrying in a Candle's Flame

When you wish to use fire scrying, it is helpful to connect with the flame spirit fire faery in order to boost your success. This is also a good exercise to connect with fire faeries in general. Light a beeswax or red candle, and after it has been burning for a few moments and the flame is steady, relax and try to feel the rhythm of the flame. It is hard to explain in words, but when you feel it, you'll know. When you are ready, chant this spell and scry in the flame:

I feel the rhythm and the heat,

Spirit of fire, your help I seek.

I connect with the heartbeat of the candle's glow,

To glimpse a sign of my future shown.

Gaze into the flame with relaxed vision and note what images are seen either in the flame or in your mind's eye. Take notes.

Michael Furie

NOTES:

July 8
Tuesday

2nd ♏

☽ v/c 6:32 pm

☽ → ♐ 9:24 pm

Color of the day: Red
Incense of the day: Cedar

Thunderstorms

In the Northern Hemisphere, summer is truly upon us, and with it comes increased thunderstorm activity. A thunderstorm calls forth each of the four elements: air, water, fire, and earth. The next time there is a thunderstorm, take time to closely observe it, being careful not to place anyone in danger. Turn out the lights. (They may go out anyway.) In a fireproof container, burn a large candle in the color of your choice, for whatever your intention. Open the curtains or blinds, and settle down in a comfortable spot where you are not too close to the windows, but are able to see the sky. Allow yourself to become entranced by the storm, and meditate on the power of the elements. Wind blows—intention. Rain falls—blessing. Lightning strikes—energy. Thunder reverberates—closure.

Air, Water, Fire, and Earth,

East, West, South, and North,

I ask of the elements and corners four,

Protection provide from this storm at my door.

I pause in my actions, freely lost

In this space and time, nature tossed.

I reflect on _____, till storm is done,

With positive intentions, harm to none.

Emyme

NOTES:

July 9
Wednesday

2nd ♐

Color of the day: Yellow
Incense of the day: Bay laurel

Sparkling Insights

At this time of year, sparklers and other fireworks are readily available. Sometimes you can even find them in different elemental colors. Fire elementals particularly love these things, which are showy but fairly safe if you take reasonable precautions. Different kinds of light may reveal subtly different details about the inner or outer world. The brief, brilliant light of sparklers is good for catching sudden insights.

Obtain a package of sparklers, ideally in a variety of colors. Stick them in the ground, one at a time, and light them. As you burn each one, say:

Sparkling light,

Catch and take flight.

Burn in the air;

Show me what's there.

Truth lives in flame,

Sure as a name.

Here and then gone,

Thought lingers on.

Watch for ideas to appear in the quick flickering light and shadow of the sparklers.

Elizabeth Barrette

NOTES:

July 10
Thursday

2nd ♐

☽ v/c 8:19 pm

☽ → ♑ 11:24 pm

Color of the day: Purple
Incense of the day: Nutmeg

Meeting the Challenge

Are you facing an arduous task or challenge? Do a ritual of empowerment to speed you along the way. Begin at dawn—the best time for fresh starts. Before beginning, make a detailed list of each step that you must complete to meet the challenge. Now ground, center, and invoke the elements—or use whatever ritual structure suits your purposes. Set a piece of snowflake obsidian (a powerful grounding stone) on your altar, and allow it to charge throughout your ritual. Set your detailed list on the altar as well. Explain aloud the challenges you face, asking for guidance:

May I have the strength of earth, inspiration of air, passions of fire, and flexibility of water.

Tie a red string around your wrist as a symbol of power. Conclude the ritual, tucking the stone into your pocket and leaving the list and string in place until your goals are met.

Susan Pesznecker

July 11
Friday

2nd ♑

Color of the day: Coral
Incense of the day: Violet

Beautification Motivation

It's an excellent day for focused efforts related to beautification. Since everything is connected, beautifying your body and/or home will in turn help beautify every area of your life. Light a white candle. Say:

This is the light of motivation and unbending intent.

Light a pink candle. Say:

This is the light of divine beauty.

Place your left hand on your heart and your right hand on your belly. Say:

Effort begets blessings, blessings beget beauty, beauty begets more beauty, and on and on it goes. Aphrodite, beloved goddess, as I take steps to enhance my attractiveness and that of my home, please bolster my motivation and infuse my results with your radiant glow.

Next, brainstorm a list of proactive beautifying steps you might take in the physical realm: give yourself a facial or manicure, take regular morning jogs, clear clutter, mend the curtains. Act on at least one of them today.

Tess Whitehurst

July 12
Saturday

2nd ♑

☽ull Moon in ♑ 7:25 am

☽ v/c 9:56 pm

☽ → ♒ 11:07 pm

Color of the day: Brown
Incense of the day: Sage

As Simple as Nature

Today the full moon falls on the birthday of Henry David Thoreau, who said in his book *Walden*:

"Let us first be as simple and well as Nature ourselves, dispel the clouds which hang over our brows, and take up a little life into our pores."

Go out where you can see the moon. Ask the moon for guidance in finding a deeper, simpler connection to nature.

Go to the east. Ask the east to show you its elements. Listen to east.

Go to the south. Ask the south to show you its elements. Listen to south.

Go to the west. Ask the west to show you its elements. Listen to west.

Go to the north. Ask the north to show you its elements. Listen to north.

Stand in the center and ask nature to guide you in her simplicity and knowledge.

Thank nature. Thank the elements. Thank the moon.

Deborah Lipp

NOTES:

July 13
Sunday

3rd ♒

Color of the day: Orange
Incense of the day: Heliotrope

Citrus for Prosperity

The solar energetic vibrations that rule over Sunday conjure images of golden yellow and orange hues, making it a perfect day to focus on boosting prosperity in the home.

Gather a large, attractive bowl; several golden-colored citrus fruits, such as oranges or tangerines; your prosperity incense of choice; and an image of the Hotei Buddha (the laughing Buddha). Place the Hotei image and the oranges in the bowl on your dining table. The dining table often serves as an energetic center of the home, as family members often gather here for spiritual nourishment (socialization and interaction) and bodily nourishment (meals). Light your incense, hold your hands over the bowl of citrus, and charge with the following incantation:

By auspicious fruit of golden peel,

I make this humble appeal:

Health, Wealth, and Prosperity,

May your golden light shine upon my home and family.

For the highest good,
So mote it be.

Blake Octavian Blair

July 14
Monday

3rd ♒

☽ v/c 3:23 pm

☽ → ♓ 10:40 pm

Color of the day: White
Incense of the day: Rosemary

Surviving Monday Morning Frazzles

Monday morning can be a shock to the system of any good worker. We never know what to expect when we arrive at our place of business. Aromatherapy can keep us away from panic or stress and put us on the right track to solve even the most difficult of work tasks.

Smells are critical to our well-being. Smells can excite, calm, comfort, or invigorate us. We should learn to use smells to help us cope with stress in our everyday life. Aromatherapy has been shown to decrease stress and promote calm, among other benefits.

Use essential oils, as they are pure, and be sure to test for allergies before using. For calm and stress reduction, you can use lavender, cedar wood, patchouli, sandalwood, or rose. To invigorate, use oils of orange, peppermint, rosemary, or lemongrass.

Boudica

July 15
Tuesday

3rd ♓

Color of the day: Gray
Incense of the day: Basil

Runic Protection

Runes often come to mind when dealing with protection spells and sigils. Perhaps it's the grace inherent in their alphabet. Whatever the reason, the runes were certainly the inspiration for this home protection spell.

For this spell, you'll need air-hardening clay of some sort and a tool to etch a symbol into your clay—a toothpick will work just fine. Soften and knead the clay before dividing it into four balls, each about the size of a cherry tomato. Squish each ball into a flat disc. Now, you want to etch a protective rune into each disk. Options include Ken (protection of valuables), Othel (heirlooms, possessions, home, and land), or even Thor's hammer. Allow to dry and then consecrate the discs to the protection of your home. Finally, bury one at each corner of the house or property.

Laurel Reufner

 ## July 16
Wednesday

3rd ♓

☽ v/c 8:57 pm

Color of the day: Brown
Incense of the day: Lavender

Mighty Brigid of the Flame

Here is a spell to help banish an ailment or illness that calls upon the Irish goddess Brigid—a lady of poetry, smithcraft, the returning spring, sovereignty of the land, and healing and health.

Light a candle, if you have one handy, or call upon the element of fire. This spell may be cast for yourself or another with their knowledge.

Chant the following while committing to health and balance:

Mighty Brigid of the flame,

I call to you in your name,

Keep me (or name) healthy,

Keep me (or name) whole,

In mind, in body, in heart, in soul.

Gede Parma

July 17
Thursday

3rd ♓

☽ → ♈ 12:07 am

Color of the day: Turquoise
Incense of the day: Balsam

harness the Sun

The sun is high and the days are long, so why not harness the power of the sun and channel it toward adding some extra protection energy to your home?

Plant marigolds in a circle, in your yard or in a round pot. Right in the center of the marigolds, stick a solar light. Here's a charm to awaken the sun's energy and activate your protective flowers:

Lovely flowers circle round,

The sun's bright energy abound.

Protect my property day and night,

And bless my home with stored sunlight.

The sun will shine on your new solar shield all day, and the power of the sun will radiate from the solar light in the night, vigilantly keeping watch and deflecting negative energy.

Mickie Mueller

July 18
Friday

3rd ♈

Fourth Quarter 10:08 pm

☽ v/c 10:18 pm

Color of the day: Purple
Incense of the day: Rose

Isn't It lovely?

It's a Friday night in summer. Love should be in the air, and if it's not, use this spell to help draw it in.

If you have a little rose water or rose oil, add it to your pulse points. Recite this spell, and either entice your partner into the bedroom if you already have one, or get out there in the world and find yourself one!

The love I want,

The love I need,

Please let love

Return to me.

Moon above,

Pale and white,

Draw to me my love

On this summer night.

Kerri Connor

July 19
Saturday

4th ♈

☽ → ♉ 4:43 am

Color of the day: Blue
Incense of the day: Pine

Invisible Workers

We are surrounded by invisible people. Not just the fairies and little people, but the people working behind the scenes providing services that help us everywhere we go. They make our lives easier, make traffic flow, and keep people safe and cared for. They are the hands that set the coffee in front of us at a restaurant, the maids who make up hotel rooms, the bus driver, the crosswalk guard, and even the guy who loads us onto the ferris wheel at the fair— invisible workers.

Put on your magical eyes, and today, see and bless these invisible workers. Look for the people behind the scenes. Look into their eyes, smile, and thank them. Initiate conversations with the street sweeper, the utility repair person, and the grocery clerk. When you look them in the eye and thank them, something magical happens. Suddenly they are no longer invisible.

Dallas Jennifer Cobb

July 20
Sunday

4th ♉

Color of the day: Gold
Incense of the day: Marigold

Ritual of honoring Women

Today marks the 166th anniversary of the first women's rights convention in the United States. Take some time to think about all those who suffered in order to win women their rights today, women (and some men!) who changed not only the Unites States, but who changed the world. Watch "Iron Jawed Angels," the story of Alice Paul, through whose courage and determination women finally got the right to vote in the United States.

Hold a deep blue candle while meditating on the female energies of receptivity, endurance, and bear-like protectiveness ... then ponder the male side of protectiveness, too, as well as those of action and drive. Say a prayer of gratitude to the Lord and the Lady, to all the women and men who have paved the way for women, and determine what you will do to keep the road passable to those who follow you.

Now carve a field of stars, embellishing them with some glitter or sparkly paint, if you like, for the dark and light energies that create balance. Light this candle whenever you feel especially grateful for the rights of women everywhere.

Thuri Calafia

NOTES:

July 21
Monday

♃ ☿ ♉
☽ v/c 10:12 am
☽ → ♊ 12:36 pm

Color of the day: Ivory
Incense of the day: Narcissus

The Cingulum

A cingulum, in magickal terms, is a cord that encircles one's waist. It may be purely decorative—tied around a robe or tunic—or, more often, it may signify rank or accomplishment. Different traditions suggest different colors for the cord; green is often used for neophytes, and red or black for those of "rank."

You can design your own cingulum, using colors appropriate for your own traditions and practices. A traditional length of cord is equal to your own height, or you might prefer a cord of special length, such as nine feet—useful for laying out a magick circle. Always tie the cingulum using a square knot: this four-sided knot is supremely strong and also references the four elements and a sense of symmetry and balance. Use the cingulum to mark steps in your work by braiding in new colors or using intricate knot work.

Susan Pesznecker

July 22
Tuesday

♃ ♊
☉ → ♌ 5:41 pm

Color of the day: Maroon
Incense of the day: Geranium

Tarot Spell for Success

Gather cinnamon oil; red, orange, and yellow candles; and the tarot cards Strength and the Sun. Anoint the candles with cinnamon oil, and place the red candle on the left side of your altar, the orange candle in the middle, and the yellow candle on the right side. Place the Strength card in between the red and orange candles on the left, and place the Sun card between the orange and yellow candles on the right. This way, you will draw in strength and project successful energy. Next, visualize being successful at your chosen endeavor. Now, light the red candle and say:

Power of fire, feed my spirit.

Light the orange candle and say:

Power of the Sun, shine good fortune upon me.

Light the yellow candle and say:

Strength and fortune here combine; ensure success shall now be mine!

Allow the candles to burn for at least one hour.

Michael Furie

July 23
Wednesday

4th ♊

☽ v/c 8:53 pm
☽ → ♋ 10:59 pm

Color of the day: White
Incense of the day: Marjoram

Neptunalia

In ancient Rome, a festival on this day honored Neptune. While Neptune's origins are shrouded in mystery, at some point his identity merged with that of the Greek Poseidon, the trident-wielding god of the sea. Neptune/Poseidon is a powerful deity: his alignment with the waters indicates his association with treasure and prosperity, and his plethora of divine children indicates his potent fertility magic.

Create an altar to Neptune today. Perhaps include his image, some seashells, a chalice or bowl of water, and a deep blue candle. Say:

Neptune, powerful and regal ruler of the sea, I honor you this day.

Choose a single intention or desire related to prosperity, success, or fertility, and tell Neptune about it, being sure to respectfully request his assistance with the matter. Thank him in advance for doing so, then light a stick of incense as a fragrant offering of gratitude and devotion.

Tess Whitehurst

July 24
Thursday

4th ♋

Color of the day: Green
Incense of the day: Myrrh

Dog Days of Summer

Sirius, the dog star, is most easily seen this time of year, which led the ancients to believe he was the cause of the hot, sultry weather often experienced from July 24 to August 24 (in the Northern Hemisphere).

During these dog days, we are encouraged to remember our canine companions and pets in general. Remember to keep lots of water available. Do not leave pets outside too long, and never ever leave a pet in a car, even with the windows cracked. For those who have no pets, please consider making a donation or money or supplies to a local pet shelter or animal rescue organization.

Take a few moments before you retire this night to send out good and positive energy for all the creatures of the earth.

Emyme

July 25

Friday

4ħ ♋

☽ v/c 9:53 am

Color of the day: Pink
Incense of the day: Thyme

Changing Times

When they think of money, most people think of cash. Today, most people carry money in the form of credit cards, debit cards, gift cards, or similar symbols of stored money. So it's important to update magical practice to keep pace with these social and economic changes.

For this spell, you'll need a Ziploc bag and an old money card (old, because these cards usually have a magnetic strip, and magical energy can mess with magnetic energy—it's the symbolism of the card that counts). Hold the card and meditate on your prosperity. Then close it in the bag, saying:

Shield my money,

Safe and sound,

From all hazards

That are found.

Hold it fast and

Help it grow

As the magics

Round it flow.

Keep the bagged card in a safe place, such as on your altar.

Elizabeth Barrette

Notes:

July 26
Saturday

4th ♋
☽ → ♌ 10:55 am
New Moon in ♌ 6:42 pm
Color of the day: Black
Incense of the day: Ivy

A New Moon Cleansing Spell

This new moon cleansing spell uses pennyroyal as a powerful purifier. Pennyroyal has the magical ability to stop arguments, so it was called the herb of peace. And if pennyroyal is near, it repels the evil eye.

Pennyroyal should be at its peak now in the July garden. Pick three stems of pennyroyal and dip them into saltwater. Using the stems as a sprinkler, sprinkle the saltwater at all exterior doors. When done, discard the stems; the oil in the leaves can be toxic, so dispose of them in the trash—you don't want a pet to eat them.

Next, using your ritual broom, sweep each threshold vigorously away from your home and toward the curb. As you sweep, say this:

Pennyroyal, the herb of peace,

Thank you for cleansing my home.

All discord will now cease.

James Kambos

 ## July 27
Sunday

1st ♌
☽ v/c 8:37 pm
Color of the day: Yellow
Incense of the day: Almond

Good Luck Floor Wash

A magical floor wash is a great way to wash away negative energies lingering around your home and welcome good luck. Bring a big pot of water to boil, and add a few slices of lemon and some rosemary, lavender, sea salt, and basil. While you wait for the solution to cool, mop your floors with your usual cleaners. You may charge it with this charm:

My magical floor wash,
I empower this very second,
minute, and hour.

Empty your bucket and then fill it with your brew, adding some white vinegar and water to top it off. Now do a final mop with the floor wash, making sure to get the corners.

Sometimes I like to reserve a cup of the liquid before I mop and put it in a spray bottle so that I can mist it on the cabinets, doors, windows, or any place that needs an extra good-luck boost.

Mickie Mueller

July 28
Monday

1st ♌

☽ → ♍ 11:37 pm

Color of the day: Lavender
Incense of the day: Lily

Declaration of Independence

Commemorate the Peruvian declaration of independence from Spanish conquistadors. This spell helps you list what you wish to have independence from—bad habits, toxic relationships, stress, or debt—and plan a path toward freedom.

Independence doesn't happen overnight. Like the Peruvians, you'll have to plan, strategize, organize, and fight for your rights. First make your list. Then choose one thing and write it on a separate paper. For example: *Eliminate credit card debt.* Write the steps toward freedom: *Curtail credit card purchases. Use tax return to pay off Visa. Use birthday money to pay down MasterCard.* Attach dates to each step, and identify a final date for independence. *Clear debts by June.* Fold plan in half, and state: *I declare my independence.* Fold it in half again. *Self determination is my right.*

Place your independence plan on your altar and revisit it as needed until you are free. Do this for each of your wishes.

Dallas Jennifer Cobb

July 29
Tuesday

1st ♍

Color of the day: Gray
Incense of the day: Ylang-ylang

A Tiger's-Eye View of Passion

Today is International Tiger Day. This day is dedicated to raising awareness for tiger conservation. In many cultures the tiger symbolizes passion. Today, consider the importance of helping to save this magnificent animal, and call upon the energy of the tiger to regain focus of and renew the spark for your passions in life.

Find a tiger's-eye stone and hold it to your third eye chakra. Concentrate on your passions in life, whether they be art, music, teaching, cooking, parenting, etc. As you beam the information about your passions into the stone, also draw in the vibrant, motivating energy of the tiger's-eye.

When finished, either carry the stone on your person or keep it on your altar as an energetic reminder to live your life with enthusiasm and to fulfill your passions!

Blake Octavian Blair

July 30
Wednesday

1st ♍

Color of the day: Brown
Incense of the day: Honeysuckle

Religious Freedom

On this day in 1956, President Eisenhower made "In God we trust" the official motto of the United States.

This is a spell for religious freedom, to help people everywhere be free to worship the god(s) of their choice (including none), in the manner of their choice.

Set up your altar with a range of symbols for religions: pentacle, Druid sigil, Christian cross, Star of David, Islamic star and crescent, etc.

Smudge the altar with sage. Pick up each symbol to make sure it's thoroughly smudged. While doing this, chant the word *freedom*, focusing intently on the concept.

When ready to release the spell, toss confetti over the altar, shouting:

We are free! So mote it be!

Send donations to charities of your choice that work for human rights in the U.S. or abroad, enclosing a bit of the confetti in each envelope.

Deborah Lipp

July 31
Thursday

1st ♍

☽ v/c 10:47 am
☽ → ♎ 12:09 pm

Color of the day: White
Incense of the day: Carnation

Success in an Enterprise

Today is the birthday of the J. K. Rowling character of great fame, Harry Potter. With a bit of pop-culture magic, here is a way to work with the egregore and spirit of Harry Potter to summon success in our endeavors and enterprises.

Find an image of Harry Potter; one in which he is personifying the energy of success, which so often leads him and his friends to triumph and victory.

Ground, center, and align. Gaze at the image of HP and feel how you are becoming invested with his strength of success. Feel how this will lead you to triumph in your enterprise!

Chant the following to seal the spell:

Harry Potter, born on this day,

Powerful wizard, I call you here,

Lend me success and open my way,

And any blocks, with your wand clear!

Gede Parma

August

Named for Roman Emperor Augustus Caesar, August means "regal, dignified, or grand." It calls to mind the celebrations of late summer and golden fields of tall, nodding stalks of grain. It also begins the bounty of autumn. To draw the power of August into your spellcasting, use its correspondences. Its herbs include angelica, bay, chamomile, fennel, marigold, St. John's wort, and sunflower. Add grains such as barley, corn, rye, or wheat. For stones, use carnelian or jasper. Burn heliotrope or frankincense. General colors are yellow, gold, and deep green. Most deities associated with August have a certain dignity. Diana, goddess of woods and hunting, has a temple holiday on August 13. Thoth, god of writing and the moon, oversees several feasts. Then there is Lugh, a trickster and Jack-of-all-trades. Lugh celebrates this month with games and competitions. With those associations, what kind of spellcraft can you work in August? Try rituals about gathering, harvesting, or preserving. Spells for health and vitality get a boost from the strong solar energy. On a more personal note, turn to appreciation and friendship, the natural counterpoint to the love and fertility focus of spring and summer.

Elizabeth Barrette

August 1

Friday

1st ♎

☽ v/c 10:58 pm

Color of the day: Rose
Incense of the day: Cypress

Lammas

A Prayer of Thanks

On this day, the celebration of the first harvest, we need to remember to be thankful for all we have. Many of us have a bad habit of taking the abundance in our lives for granted.

During the entire harvest season, from Lammas to Samhain, think of at least one thing you are thankful for each day. As you come up with each item, say:

Great Goddess and Great Father,

Today I remember to be grateful

For the abundance in my life and

To not take it for granted.

Today I am thankful for (name whatever it is).

I thank you for bringing this into my life

And cherish the fact that I have all that I do.

Thank you, Lord and Lady, for your bountiful gifts,

Now and throughout the entire year.

Kerri Connor

 August 2

Saturday

1st ♎

☽ → ♏ 10:57 pm

Color of the day: Indigo
Incense of the day: Magnolia

Whirligig Wishes

Make some end-of-summer wishes with enchanting maple seeds. This works best if you're lucky enough to have a windy day. If not, stand on something so the whirligig can get some height to really spin away.

Hold the seed in your hand and take a deep, grounding breath, focusing on your wish. Now cup the maple seed in your hand, and softly whisper your wish to the seed. Hold the seed in your dominant hand, and fling the seed away from you, letting the wind carry your wish off to the universe. (If you don't live in an area with maple seeds, try using a beautiful leaf instead.)

Laurel Reufner

August 3
Sunday

1st ♏

Second Quarter 8:50 pm

Color of the day: Yellow
Incense of the day: Juniper

Spell for Increased Wisdom

Buy some whole hazelnuts (filberts) and place them in a bowl or cauldron. Hold both hands over the bowl, will your energy to flow into the nuts, and bless them with the following chant:

Ancient seed of wisdom and power,

I call on you to release your might.

Enliven my heart and mind each hour,

New understandings, wisdom take flight!

Eat a hazelnut when you are facing a problem or if you are studying and need a boost of brain power.

Michael Furie

NOTES:

August 4
Monday

2nd ♏

☽ v/c 1:43 pm

Color of the day: Gray
Incense of the day: Lily

Great Wardmote of the Woodmen of Arden

It can be no accident the Great Wardmote of the Woodmen of Arden takes place the first week of August, culminating on August 4. The first harvest is in. Now is the time for a little relaxation before work begins anew, leading up to the autumnal equinox. This wardmote, or community meeting, harkens back to 1785, when all the woodmen in the Forest of Arden banded together to discuss their rights and duties. Now, as then, feasting and archery contests are held. The participants dress in eighteenth-century costume.

In our modern world, August is a time of slowing down prior to the next season. Communities hold county fairs and local craft festivals. Renaissance Faires take place. Farmers' markets begin to offer pumpkins and other fall "fruits." Join in the celebration. Gather together your family or neighborhood or coven for a celebration featuring locally grown produce and old-fashioned games of skill, such as archery. Period costumes optional.

August 5
Tuesday

2nd ♏

☽ → ♐ 6:19 am

Color of the day: White
Incense of the day: Basil

Protection for Our Home

We have keys and locks, and some of us have alarms on our doors. Witches put up wards, which need to be reinforced at least annually.

I like metal nails at corners of the property. Count the corners, as not all properties are square. Bless the nails with blessed water (either by you or a priest) and walk the property, inserting the nails, point down, into the corners. As you walk the property, sprinkle salt and water to bless the edges. On top of each nail head, I also place a black stone (bags of them are available at dollar stores) anointed with a pentacle made with protection oil.

Indoors, I use the same black stones at doors and windows, usually in corners where they are discreet. Also, make pentacles with protection oil on doors, windows, and locks. You can make your own oil, or it can be purchased.

Boudica

August 6
Wednesday

2nd ♐

☽ v/c 10:52 am

Color of the day: Topaz
Incense of the day: Lavender

Blessing with Fire: The Fire Kit

Any magick user should be able to kindle fire, and this will be easier to do with a ready-to-use fire kit. Dip "strike anywhere" matches in melted paraffin or clear fingernail polish, and allow to dry; store in an empty film canister or other airtight holder. Save a large handful of laundry lint from your dryer trap, storing it in a plastic bag; this lights instantly and burns hot. Collect candle stubs and broken crayons; these melt in a fire and help wood "catch." Add a pocketknife for creating shavings and a couple tightly folded pieces of newspaper. You might also include pieces of resinous "fatwood" and a fire starter kit—these usually contain flint and steel or magnesium and steel.

Store your components in a watertight container decorated with the elemental symbol for fire: an upward-facing triangle. Each time you kindle fire, offer a blessing of thanks for this life-sustaining gift.

Susan Pesznecker

August 7
Thursday

2nd ♐

☽ → ♑ 9:38 am

Color of the day: Purple
Incense of the day: Clove

howl at the Moon!

Gather your witchy buddies together for an evening, and head for a local forest, field, or other wild setting where there's no curfew. The moon, just three days now from the full, should be rising in the evening in the Northern Hemisphere (check for details in your own region), so she's perfectly timed for a lively rite of wildness. Have a nice dinner, then take some cakes and ale out with you and your cohorts to the agreed-upon location. Tell them:

This ritual is a non-ritual. Nothing is written or planned, other than letting our wild selves out to romp. No judgment or guilt allowed.

Then set the example for them by beginning yourself with singing, stomping, clapping, drumming, chanting, or simply tipping up your chin and howling at the Lady's lustrous form. Open yourself to your wild side and allow . . . run, dance, skip, jump, act like a fool. Get drunk on her moonshine, and be blessed!

Thuri Calafia

August 8
Friday

2nd ♑

Color of the day: Coral
Incense of the day: Vanilla

Inner Thirst

In Japan, August 7th and 8th are known as "dog days," and in much of North America we refer to this hot, sultry time of year as the "dog days of summer."

Today, while quenching your bodily thirst, attend to your inner thirst. Assemble these salty, sweet, bitter, and neutral elements: a pinch of salt, three tablespoons sugar, the juice of one lemon, and a glass of cold water. Combine all and stir well. The pinch of salt ensures replenishment of minerals lost through sweat. Bless the concoction with intent:

Neutral, salty, sour, and sweet, in this drink these all meet.

With these I nurture my inner fire, and do what's needed to accomplish desires.

Drink to replenish body and soul. Then do one small thing that satisfies your inner thirst, moving you toward your heart's desire.

Dallas Jennifer Cobb

August 9
Saturday

2nd ♑

☽ v/c 4:09 am
☽ → ♒ 9:52 am

Color of the day: Black
Incense of the day: Sandalwood

International Day of the World's Indigenous People

Thanks to the United Nations, today is a day for raising awareness about the world's numerous populations of indigenous people. As Pagans, we draw our inspiration from the indigenous way of life, which may be broadly described as a reverence of nature and a respect for the interconnection between everything in the natural world.

So today, honor the indigenous roots of your spiritual and/or cultural heritage. For example, if you're Irish or have Celtic aspects to your spiritual practice, you might spend some time with an oak today: pour a libation of ale around her roots and remember your ancient connection with this magical being. Or if you're Native American or resonate with Native American spirituality, you might go outside and lovingly offer a pinch of tobacco to the four directions. You'll find that even simple acts like these can realign you with a vast wellspring of wisdom and inspiration.

Tess Whitehurst

August 10

Sunday

2nd ♒

Full Moon in ♒ 2:09 pm

☽ v/c 6:12 pm

Color of the day: Gold
Incense of the day: Eucalyptus

August Abundance Spell

The August full moon, the Grain Moon, rises over the horizon tonight and shines with a reddish glow. It rides above a world of late summer bounty. The Grain Moon's spells and rituals should focus on sharing, caring, and giving thanks.

Ideally, this ritual should be worked with a coven or a like-minded friend. Food banks run low at this time of year, so begin a day ahead and tell coven members to bring a nonperishable food item. Include the food items as part of your altar decorations, along with seasonal flowers, a yellow candle, and a dish of cornmeal.

Begin the ritual outside, and have the leader raise the cornmeal silently toward the moon. Pass the dish, and have each member mention something they're grateful for—let each person sprinkle a bit of the cornmeal on the ground. Return to the altar and light the candle.

Together say:

*Thank you, Grain Moon,
for your blessings.*

We will share because we care.

The next day, deliver your food to your local food bank.

James Kambos

NOTES:

August 11

Monday

3rd ♒

☽ → ♓ 8:55 am

Color of the day: Silver
Incense of the day: Hyssop

Row by Row

Autumn is the season of harvest, which typically begins in early August. Previously done with draft horses or oxen, it involves cutting the grain and turning over the earth. This is now done primarily with tractors, but it still entails going back and forth over the rows. So harvest is a time of repetition and introspection. This lends itself well to meditation.

Any kind of repetitious, back-and-forth motion is suitable for this meditation. Knitting, crocheting, raking leaves in the yard, or even walking will work. Choose what you can do, what helps settle your mind. Seek to attune yourself to the energy of the harvest season. As you go back and forth, repeat this mantra:

As the ox plows,

As the tractor turns,

Row by row,

As the pen writes,

As the knitter binds,

Row by row,

So time passes

And minds remember,

Seasons go.

Elizabeth Barrette

NOTES:

August 12
Tuesday

3rd ♓

☽ v/c 12:01 pm

Color of the day: Maroon
Incense of the day: Ginger

Faerie Garden Blessing

Call upon the faeries, the Fey, the Wild Ones of Nature, to bless your garden with this simple spell.

Consider the fact that if you live outside of Europe, and you yourself are of some European descent, the fey ones you call may be both European faerie and native-to-the-land Fey. This is a crucial understanding. To learn more about the relationships between migratory spirits and indigenous spirits of place, read Charles de Lint's *Newford* series.

Lay out sweet offerings of organic honey, cacao, nectar, and perhaps dairy milk if you are keen on the European faeries as well.

Sing and shake bells in the center of your garden to call in the Good Neighbors:

Come, blessed Wild Ones,

Here to this garden,

Laid here are offerings,

For you to take in.

Come, blessed faeries,

Here to this garden,

I sing for your honor,

Inviting you in.

Gede Parma

NOTES:

August 13

Wednesday

3rd ♓

☽ → ♈ 9:00 am

Color of the day: Yellow
Incense of the day: Honeysuckle

Death Card Tarot Meditation

The number thirteen has been severely maligned in popular culture and by many "mainstream" religions. However, it is a sacred number to Witches, and in honor of this being the thirteenth day of the month, here is a meditation using the thirteenth major arcana card of the tarot.

Pull the Death card from your favorite tarot deck, then place the card on your altar and light your favorite meditation incense. Meditate upon the Death card's meaning: radical change, rebirth, the old giving way to the new. The calendar year is now more than half over. What changes have you experienced or are you currently undergoing? What will be the new growth from the death of the old? Change can be difficult and sometimes painful; however, it is important to recognize its affirmative effects. When finished, journal about your experience.

Blake Octavian Blair

August 14

Thursday

3rd ♈

Color of the day: Green
Incense of the day: Jasmine

Virtual Money Manifestation

Try this spell to bring in money for something specific that you need. You'll need digital images of your need, as well as either digital scrapbooking or imaging software. (I use MyMemories.)

Mentally prepare yourself for spellcasting. You might wish to light a white candle nearby. Work on creating your scrapbook page up to the point where you have the background papers in place. Take a moment to create some word art stating your need. This is the next component to go on your page. Finish up by placing the photos and adding whatever embellishments you wish. The word area should be completely hidden behind the images. That forms the hidden intent of the magic. When embellishing, remember to keep the focus on your need.

Finally, either print the finished page or set it as wallpaper on your computer. Take a moment each day to see your need fulfilled.

Laurel Reufner

August 15
Friday

3rd ♈

☽ v/c 11:50 am

☽ → ♉ 11:58 am

Color of the day: Pink
Incense of the day: Violet

Cat Protection Amulet

Those of us who have cats love them very much. Cats are sacred to the goddess Freya, who adored her cats, and Friday is named for Freya. If you have a cat that roams outdoors, here's a spell to make a protection amulet. You'll need a small amulet of amber, jade, or moonstone; it doesn't need to be large or expensive and shouldn't be longer than a tag on your cat's collar—a lone earring would work. Rub sandalwood oil on the amulet, and place it next to a white candle. Light the candle and charge the amulet:

Freya, I charge this amulet in your name,

Watch over my cat with your blessed flame.

Keep her/him safe be it day or night,

Be it under the sun or the pale moonlight.

Once the candle burns down, clip the amulet to your cat's collar.

Mickie Mueller

 August 16
Saturday

3rd ♉

Color of the day: Brown
Incense of the day: Sage

Letting Go of Memories

Does something from the past haunt you? Use the waning moon to help banish memories.

Gather items that evoke memories. Lay a square of black cotton, large enough to wrap up all your memory objects, flat on your altar.

Meditate on the past. Feel it as a weight inside you. Imagine it growing lighter and lighter, floating up like a bubble. Let it rise and disappear.

One by one, hold each item. Say:

I am ready to let you go.
I can forget you now.

Place the item on the cloth.

Pull the corners of the cloth together to form a bag. Tie it with a silver cord. Leave a long end to carry the bag.

Find a bridge, preferably over running water. Hold the bag by the cord. Say:

I let you go. I forget you.

Cut the cord and let the bag fall into the water. Don't look back.

Deborah Lipp

August 17
Sunday

3rd ♉

Fourth Quarter 8:26 am

☽ v/c 8:26 am

☽ → ♊ 6:41 pm

Color of the day: Amber
Incense of the day: Heliotrope

Sacrifices

Sunday is a day to celebrate the strength and boldness of the God. It is on this particular Sunday that we honor Odin for the beginning of his ordeal on the world tree Yggdrasil, which led to his discovery of the runes.

Gods, kings, and tribal chiefs have often made great sacrifices for their people. What kind of sacrifice can you make in return? We no longer sacrifice things such as animals to show our appreciation, so what can you sacrifice instead to show your dedication? Meditate on this question until you find your answer.

Some people sacrifice their time by spending time in prayer or helping others in the name of their God. Some "come out of the closet" as a sacrifice—they give up their privacy to show others they are proud of their God and their pathway. What will you sacrifice to show your God your love and respect for him?

Thuri Calafia

August 18
Monday

4th ♊

Color of the day: Ivory
Incense of the day: Rosemary

Stop Gossip Spell

For this spell to end gossip, you'll need a small glass jar with a lid, a small piece of paper, a pinch each of salt and clove, a drop of olive oil, and a gray candle.

Begin by blending together the salt, clove, and oil. Write the gossip or rumor on the paper, and apply a drop of the oil mixture to the paper. Place the paper in the jar, and screw on the lid. Dress the candle with the remaining oil mixture. Light the candle, and hold the candle over the jar, letting some of the wax drip over the lid to seal it. As you do this, say:

All lies and rumors will cease,

Vicious gossip will end in peace.

After the gossip ends, throw the jar and candle away.

James Kambos

August 19

Tuesday

4th ♊

☽ v/c 10:54 pm

Color of the day: Black
Incense of the day: Bayberry

Clear the Way for Virgo

To clear out old energetic sludge and prepare for the highly organizing (and quickly approaching) period during which the Sun will be in Virgo, choose one or more little clutter-clearing projects today, and perform it/them with a great deal of intention. For example, you might plan to roll up all your loose change, clear out the medicine cabinet, organize your desk, and get all the receipts and trash out of your wallet or purse. Before you begin, light a white candle and perhaps diffuse some rosemary and/or peppermint essential oil. Say:

As my home I clear and purge,
sparkling pathways now emerge.

Seeds of clarity now I sow,
and all that's stuck begins to flow.

If you have a limited amount of time, you might set a timer for half an hour or more and then do what you can. Otherwise, complete your chosen tasks and then continue if you feel so inspired.

Tess Whitehurst

August 20

Wednesday

4th ♊

☽ → ♋ 4:45 am

Color of the day: Brown
Incense of the day: Lilac

Back to School

This is the time of year when schools are gearing up to open their doors again for the fall. For many, colleges and universities especially, classes will begin next week. If you will be shopping for or have already purchased school and dorm supplies, collect everything in one central location. Cleanse the items with a sage stick or a light sprinkle of salt, and bless them, placing emphasis on their positive powers enabling clarity and understanding in the school year. Place a small container of honey on your altar, and light small red and yellow candles for Saraswati, the Hindu goddess of academic knowledge, science, music, and art.

Saraswati, bless these tools of enlightenment.

Bestow delight in learning and clarity in understanding.

Emyme

August 21
Thursday

4th ♋

☽ v/c 3:34 pm

Color of the day: White
Incense of the day: Apricot

Releasing Stress Through a Tree

When you are really stressed, it is helpful to use a tree to help ground you and relieve the stressful energy from your body. To do this, find a strong tree and sit at its base with your back leaning against the tree trunk. Breathe slowly and deeply and allow the tree to draw the harmful energy right out of you. In order to avoid polluting the tree's energy with undo stress, you can recite this spell to help focus the transformation of the energy, thus freeing you while keeping the tree safe (you and the tree are the "we" in the spell):

Ancient tree, reaching down through earth and up to the stars,

Scatter this stress, scatter it far.

Recycle the chaos; we're free from this storm

And left with inner quiet and calm.

When you feel better, thank the tree before you leave.

Michael Furie

 August 22
Friday

4th ♋

☽ → ♌ 4:49 pm

Color of the day: Purple
Incense of the day: Orchid

End-of-Week Love Myself Working

Congratulations! You made it through another week. Do you reward yourself for your persistence in the face of adversity?

If you don't have a date, then make one—with yourself. We live in stressful times, when the cell phone is on 24/7 and we can be contacted by work or involved in family or friend drama.

Turn off the cell. No, not vibrate! Just shut it off. Really! No interruptions! Take the night off.

Start with a movie or two and some take-out. Move on to pink candles and a relaxing bath soak in your favorite smells. How about a relaxing glass of wine, or your favorite drink? Finally, relax in bed with soft music and your favorite book or magazine till you fall asleep. You will be surprised how much better you will feel in the morning! This kind of personal attention works magic.

Boudica

August 23

Saturday

4th ♌

☉ → ♍ 12:46 am

Color of the day: Blue

Incense of the day: Patchouli

A Peach Stone Divination

Now that peaches are in season, this is a fun form of divination to try. You'll need three clean, dry peach stones, a black marker or black craft paint, and a small basket.

Color or paint one side of each peach stone black. To answer a yes/no question, the black side represents "no" and the noncolored side represents "yes." Place all the stones in a basket, then ask your question and shake the basket. If all three black sides face up, the answer is no. If two black sides face up, the answer is likely to be no. If all three natural sides face up, it's a yes. Two natural sides facing up indicates your wish will probably come true, but you may face an obstacle. Bless your stones and keep them wrapped in a black or blue cloth when not in use.

James Kambos

August 24

Sunday

4th ♌

☽ v/c 4:26 am

Color of the day: Orange
Incense of the day: Frankincense

Spell to halt Gossip

This last sliver of moon can be used as Hecate's Sickle, bright and sharp, cutting the threads of slander and innuendo. Write the words of your accuser(s), even if that accuser is you, on a piece of parchment. Inscribe a black taper with protective symbols and phrases, such as "This ends now!" Light a charcoal, and sprinkle it with slippery elm as you read aloud the gossip and lies. Allow your rage to build, alternating the accusations with your own truths. As the energy peaks, yell:

> This is a lie, and your gossip ends
> NOW!

Fire the energy into the paper, and then light the paper with the black candle and watch it burn.

Allow your rage to dissipate, knowing that the false accusations will stop directly. Feast on red juice or wine and a favorite cookie for your cakes and wine, and let the candle burn down naturally, if safe to do so. Remember, always, the power of the word, and commit to being impeccable with yours.

Thuri Calafia

August 25

Monday

4th ♌

☽ → ♍ 5:33 am

New Moon in ♍ 10:13 am

Color of the day: Lavender
Incense of the day: Clary sage

Discover a Secret

Use this spell when something hidden causes trouble, whether on the job, at home, or in relationships.

You will need a black candle, a candle holder, and a shiny penny.

Perform the spell outdoors at night. Pray to the Lady of the Dark Moon. Say:

As the moon is revealed in light, so the secret will be revealed to me.

Hold the penny up. Say:

Like a lucky penny, knowledge appears.

Place the penny in the candle holder. Place the candle on it and light the candle. Say:

Burn away the darkness, burn away the blackness, reveal the truth.

Pray again to the Lady, asking her help in revealing this secret.

Meditate on the candle. Leave it outside where it can burn undisturbed.

In the morning, retrieve the penny. Carry it with you at all times until the full moon, then toss it away. The secret will be revealed.

Deborah Lipp

Notes:

August 26

Tuesday

1st ♍

☽ v/c 10:29 pm

Color of the day: Gray
Incense of the day: Cedar

Working with the Chalice

The chalice is a cup or vessel used for drinking sacred beverages—typically wine, mead, juice, or ale in Pagan ceremonies, although I've known friends to use herbal infusions, coffee, or even hot chocolate as well. The chalice may be simple or ornate; carved, decorated, or plain; and of wood, metal, or some other material. I love to be spontaneously creative with my chalices; for example, a "holey stone" will hold liquid in its depressions, while a seashell makes a perfect oceanside chalice.

Cleanse your chalice with the four elements: a sprinkle of saltwater and a pass through smoke over a flame. Charge it by exposure to sunlight or moonlight, and store it wrapped in a sumptuous cloth. When you use your chalice, honor it with these words:

Sacred vessel,

Borne to lips,

Share with me

Your sacred gifts.

Susan Pesznecker

August 27

Wednesday

1st ♍

☽ → ♎ 5:54 pm

Color of the day: White
Incense of the day: Bay laurel

Water Blessing

On this day historically, Romans honored Volturnus, god of waters and fountains, with feasting, wine drinking, and games. Locate a suitable body of water, something you can stand in. If you live in a city, find a pool or fountain. If you live in the country, find a lake, river, or stream. Take a picnic of bread, cheese, and wine. Enjoy an early-evening dinner by the water. Satiated, take off your shoes and socks and stand or lie in the water. Then say:

From the earth, this sacred water,

Touched by sun, cleansed by fire.

Scoop up a handful of water, and blow on it. Say:

Caressed by air and blessed by breath,

Volturnus, be blessed.

This spot is made magical. You have invoked Volturnus and can return here anytime to honor the god of waters and fountains.

Dallas Jennifer Cobb

August 28
Thursday

1st ♎

Color of the day: Crimson
Incense of the day: Mulberry

Connecting with Earth Goddess Energy

The Roman earth goddess Ops was celebrated with great revelry this time of year. The abundant fertility of all crops that grow from the earth's soil are Ops' domain.

Modern Pagans honor Mother Earth in many forms across many cultures. Take today as an opportunity to connect with the energy of the earth goddess. Go outside to a grassy area where you can sit undisturbed for a few moments. Sit directly upon the earth and feel yourself connecting to it. Commune with the earth and feel its qualities of grounding, stability, and growth well up within you. This is the energy that springs forth and nurtures all that grows from the earth's soil. Put your hands upon the earth, express your gratitude for the earth goddess's support and her abundant gifts, and send your prayers and blessings into Mother Earth. Meditate quietly until you are ready to resume the activities of the day.

Blake Octavian Blair

August 29
Friday

1st ♎

☽ v/c 12:00 pm

Color of the day: White
Incense of the day: Yarrow

Removing Obstacles

On Ganesh Chaturthi, people honor the Hindu god Ganesh. Clay statues of the elephant-headed god are displayed in tents and temples. People make offerings of coconut, jaggery sugar, red flowers, and other sacrificial items. There is dancing and singing. At the end of the festival, the statue is immersed in the river or sea so that Ganesh may return to his celestial home, taking with him the misfortunes of humanity. This is part of his purpose as the Remover of Obstacles.

Anyone can join the festivities from home. Place an image of Ganesh on your altar, and put some red flowers in a vase. Take a cleansing bath. Then tell Ganesh about your misfortunes and ask him to carry them away. Finish with the traditional closing for this occasion:

Ganapathi Bappa Morya, Purchya Varshi Laukariya.

(O father Ganesha, Come again early next year.)

Elizabeth Barrette

August 30
Saturday

1st ♎︎

☽ → ♏︎ 4:53 am

Color of the day: Black
Incense of the day: Rue

Simple Money Spell

Light a green and/or gold candle. Breathe, ground, and center, and align. Cast the circle, if you so desire.

Chant the following incantation over and over to raise the power and then release it into the candle, so that as the candle burns down, the spell potentizes.

By all the powers of three times three,

Money will come creatively.

It will pour through every crack,

To come to me and banish lack!

I conjure prosperity and make it mine,

And I do this by my power divine.

Come to me, money, and banish lack,

Prosperity pours through every crack!

Gede Parma

August 31
Sunday

1st ♏︎

Color of the day: Gold
Incense of the day: Hyacinth

Spider Weaver Spell

The first reaction many people have when they find a spider in their home is to squish it. Spiders are powerful totems. They are a symbol of the creation of life itself and also a representation of communication and connection to all things. A spider can help you weave your destiny.

If you find a lone spider in your home, catch it under a glass and carefully slide a piece of cardstock under the glass so you can carry it outside. Before you release it into your garden or a nearby tree or bush, whisper to it:

Spider friend, you'll be happier here,

I release you here without fear.

As your weaving starts to spread,

Please weave this wish into your web.

Let the spider free. As you watch it, whisper a big goal you're trying to reach to the spider. As you work toward your goal, rest assured that your new friend will be working on your behalf!

Mickie Mueller

September

September takes its name from the Latin prefix *sept*, meaning "seven," because until 153 BCE it was the seventh month of the then ten-month calendar. Even when the calendar changed, September kept its proud name. September is also known as Muin or Vine, the Celtic tree month that goes from September 2 to 29. The magical associations of Vine month include fertility, prosperity, and binding. Just as vines can creep into everything and bind onto outside structures, September is a month in which we creep into new environments and bind onto structures. Kids of all ages pack up and go back to school this month, back to structure and learning, tests and scores. Parents shift gears, too, imposing more structure on their kids, with earlier bedtimes and functional routines, plus falling into routines of their own: packing lunches, reviewing homework, and reading together. Like a vine in September, we hold on to new structures, climb toward new goals, and enjoy the fertile fruits of our labors. Take time to celebrate your accomplishments. Identify what you have achieved over the summer and vow to hold tightly to the structures that can support wild creativity. September is a time for all this.

Dallas Jennifer Cobb

September 1
Monday

1st ♏

☽ v/c 11:40 am

☽ → ♐ 1:17 pm

Color of the day: White
Incense of the day: Neroli

Labor Day

Farewell to Summer

In the United States, Labor Day (in addition to all its other associations) is traditionally seen as something of an unofficial shift to autumn and the darker time of the year. For example, historically, it has been designated as the last day of the year when wearing white, or straw hats, is stylistically acceptable. So today, say farewell to summer. In the morning, light a red candle and say:

Thank you, summer, for your radiant light and carefree joy. Though we part ways at the end of the day, the fondness in my heart for your light and heat waxes strong. Many blessings to you, dear season, until we meet again.

Wear something summery and prepare a summery meal. Enjoy the holiday with one or more of your favorite seasonal pastimes (and perhaps cocktails!), making sure to enjoy all your festivities as fully as you can.

Tess Whitehurst

  ## September 2
Tuesday

1st ♐

Second Quarter 7:11 am

Color of the day: Red
Incense of the day: Ylang-ylang

Kindle Your Spiritual Illumination

Today is the beginning of the Celtic month known as Muin. It is sacred to Lugh, the Celtic god of light, intellect, and spiritual illumination.

How would you define spiritual illumination? Different people may give different definitions. For some, it is attaining the highest level of enlightenment, while for others, it is being in touch with their astral guides. Whatever it means for you, is it truly something you are working toward? Is it a goal of yours that you work at daily? Is your spiritual illumination something that is in the forefront of your mind, or is it often pushed way behind everything else?

Starting today, pull the goal of spiritual illumination out of the background. Meditate on it. Work on it daily. Without working on it, your spirituality will become stagnant. Breathe new life into it. Find out what spiritual illumination truly means to you, and make it a priority to reach toward it more each and every day.

Kerri Connor

September 3
Wednesday

2nd ♐

☽ v/c 2:06 pm

☽ → ♑ 6:15 pm

Color of the day: Topaz
Incense of the day: Lilac

A Goldenrod Spell

Goldenrod is ruled by the Sun and is among the most healing of all herbs. Now goldenrod is blooming, spreading its cheerful yellow-gold flowers across meadows and along roadsides. To keep its protective energies close to you through winter, go to a place where goldenrod is blooming in the wild and cut a small bouquet. Bring it home and tie the stems together with a yellow ribbon, yarn, or raffia. Think of anything specific in your life that you'd like the goldenrod to help you with. It could be a health concern or just general well-being. Hang the bouquet upside down and away from direct sunlight to dry.

Let the goldenrod remind you of the warm, sunny days of late summer throughout the coming dark days of winter. In the spring, take the goldenrod to where you cut it and crumble it upon the earth as an offering.

James Kambos

September 4
Thursday

2nd ♑

Color of the day: Purple
Incense of the day: Balsam

Charge of the Mother Board

With respect to Doreen Valiente ...

Whenever ye have need of information,

Whenever code is needed by any deployment date,

Then shall ye assemble at a "hot spot,"

and tap my keys,

I who am Queen of all SEOs.

There shall ye seek input/output,

Ye who are fain to learn all technology,

Yet have not won its deepest operating secrets;

To these will I teach ye the secrets of TCP/IP and OSI.

And ye shall be free from viruses and malware;

And to show that ye be truly free,

You shall have all the latest versions and updates;

For I am the beauty of technology,

The interface with the stars,

The mystery of the i7 processor,

And the desired operating system in the heart of all geeks.

For behold, I am with thee from "Start";

And I am that which is attained at the end of the program.

Boudica

NOTES:

September 5

Friday

2nd ♑

☽ v/c 11:08 am

☽ → ♒ 7:59 pm

Color of the day: Coral
Incense of the day: Vanilla

Get the Job

Do this spell with a friend. Cense and sprinkle a space that will become your job interview location, and cense and sprinkle your resumé as well.

Dress in your interview clothes and have your friend dress as the boss. Conduct the interview as ritual theater. The "boss" loves your resumé and points out things about it that are especially perfect for the job. He or she asks you questions that you answer appropriately, and ends by offering you the job at an excellent salary. Set a start date and shake hands.

To perform this spell of ritual theater alone, dress as the boss and sit at a desk in consecrated space. Read the resumé, noting the best points out loud. Circle and underline important features. Say:

I'm going to hire [your name].
S/he is perfect for this job!

End either version with:

So mote it be!

Deborah Lipp

NOTES:

September 6
Saturday

2nd ♒

Color of the day: Gray
Incense of the day: Sage

Invoke Hermes for Travel

Beloved Hermes will help all those who come to him humbly, who come to him joyfully, who come to him with wit and cunning. This spell is dedicated to and inspired by my friend Luke CloudDancer.

If you are traveling a fair distance, call upon Hermes to ensure that your travel is safe, secure, swift, and successful.

Sing to Hermes, and arrange what offering you will give him once all your travels for now are complete and you return home safely.

You might like to use the following charm:

Wings upon your gorgeous feet,

O Hermes and your sacred fleet,

The clouds who dance across the skies,

In your wisdom I abide.

Aid me, Hermes, be my guide,

As I travel far and wide.

Be to me a lover kind,

Faithful by my loving side.

Be aware that Hermes loves to take human lovers.

Gede Parma

September 7

Sunday

2nd ≈

☽ v/c 1:19 pm

☽ → ♓ 7:47 pm

Color of the day: Amber
Incense of the day: Marigold

Candle Caring Spell

Here is one process for sending healing energy at any distance. You'll need a mirror, preferably round, small slips of paper, something that writes in the color green, and either a green pillar candle or a white glass novena candle (the tall candles that come in glass jars).

Write the name of the person you wish to send healing energy to on one of the small slips of paper with the green ink. If you have more than one, write each name on a separate piece of paper. Place the slips on the mirror, and set the candle on top of them.

Ground and center yourself, and light the candle. Next, individually, visualize each person you wish to help as being wrapped in healing light. Once you have the image strong in your mind, visualize the energy speeding on its way toward your intended target.

Let the candle burn for half an hour. When you extinguish the candle, mentally shut down the energy

flow as well. Otherwise, you may compromise your own health.

Laurel Reufner

Notes:

September 8

Monday

2nd ♓

🌕 Full Moon in ♓ 9:38 pm

Color of the day: Silver
Incense of the day: Narcissus

Full Moon Empowerment Rite

This rite will enhance spellwork. You will need an athame and a chalice of water. Go outside when you see the moon, holding the athame in your dominant hand and the cup in your other hand; catch the moon's reflection in the cup. Ask the Goddess to charge the water with power. Stir the water with the athame and sprinkle some water in a clockwise circle around you. Drink some of the water, then hold the athame and cup up high in salute. Closing your eyes, visualize three beams of moonlight shining down to fill your third eye, heart, and groin area with power. Say:

Gracious Goddess of the night,

I call to you, my spirit takes flight.

I ask for power to achieve my aim,

And this I shall do in your name.

(Repeat the chosen goddess name three times).

Blessed be.

You may now proceed with your spell.

Michael Furie

September 9

Tuesday

3rd ♓

☽ v/c 3:10 pm

☽ → ♈ 7:33 pm

Color of the day: Black
Incense of the day: Cinnamon

The Consciousness of Nine

Today being the ninth day of the month, this is a perfect opportunity to take a look at the magical number of nine. In numerology, nine is associated with patience, compassion, generosity, love of life, and global consciousness. Nine is our beloved number three multiplied by itself.

As we know that what we put into the world we shall receive back, try to embody the vibrations of the number nine today, and consciously interact with compassion, understanding, and generosity with at least nine people. Know that your contributions are benefiting the global consciousness and that your blessings will return to you. So mote it be!

Blake Octavian Blair

September 10
Wednesday

3rd ♈

☽ v/c 8:58 pm

Color of the day: Yellow
Incense of the day: Marjoram

Spell for Sacred Dreaming

Set up an altar to your most cherished deity on a small table at your bedside. Make a dream pillow by sprinkling a small piece of cotton batting with herbs like mugwort, rose, lavender, and others that help guide and relax a dreamer's mind. Cover with another piece of batting, and stitch the pieces together with a basting stitch. Slide this flat pillow into a dreamy-looking cotton casing, and slip it inside your pillowcase.

Say words of praise and gratitude to your chosen deity as you get ready for bed, and then, finally, ask for a sacred dream—a dream of guidance and deep instruction on what's currently happening in your life. In the morning, take some time to decide what the dream means to you, as well as how best to follow the advice of your deity. Be sure to leave the deity a love offering.

Thuri Calafia

September 11

Thursday

3rd ♈

☽ → ♉ 9:17 pm

Color of the day: Turquoise
Incense of the day: Carnation

Autumn Rains

In summer, the water table tends to drop as the rain comes less frequently. Long, hot, sunny days pull the water out of the air and earth. Autumn brings back the rain to replenish what was lost. What flows out, flows in again. The late flowers bloom, the final fruits come ripe, and the world prepares for its winter rest.

Here is a way to give thanks for the rain in autumn, whether present or forthcoming. Decorate your altar with images of fall and storms: red leaves in a river, bare trees against a gray sky, raindrops making circles in a puddle, and so forth. Welcome the rain with these words:

Coming back, coming home,

Autumn rains are calling.

Rushing down, rushing in,

Autumn rains are falling.

Fluting winds, drumming clouds,

Autumn rains are calling.

We bow down, we give thanks,

Autumn rains are falling.

Elizabeth Barrette

September 12

Friday

3rd ♉

Color of the day: White
Incense of the day: Cypress

Defenders Day

Today is the 200th anniversary of the Battle of North Point, at which the British were held back from overcoming the city of Baltimore, Maryland. During this land and sea engagement, the national anthem of the United States of America was penned by Francis Scott Key when he was detained overnight by the British in Baltimore harbor.

During the day, take some time and reflect on what it is you may need to guard, and how to secure that defense. In the evening, light three small candles in the colors of your ancestral homeland, and read the words to that country's national anthem. Allow the candles to burn down. As you drift to sleep, ask for an answer to your protection needs. Be sure to have pen and paper ready should that answer come to you in the night. In the morning, record your personal anthem of defense.

Emyme

September 13
Saturday

3rd ♉

☽ v/c 9:31 am

Color of the day: Blue
Incense of the day: Patchouli

honoring the Apple

Mid-September marks the apple harvest in my Pacific Northwest. It's a time rich with meaning, for the apple is considered sacred in many traditions. The wood is often burned in ritual fires, while the peel—if peeled in one continuous strand and tossed over the right shoulder—may be scryed to reveal one's future spouse. (Woe to the marriage plans of she who breaks the peel!) Apple cider and hard cider make wonderful ritual libations and may be sipped during a divination session to enhance psychic powers and speed entry into the netherworlds, for the apple is associated with Avalon and the hidden Celtic underlands. A wand made of apple wood—particularly one you fashion yourself—is a powerful tool for directing energy and working with the Fae. Bless your local apple trees on Twelfth Night (January 6) with a cup of wassail poured over their roots.

Susan Pesznecker

 ## September 14
Sunday

3rd ♉

☽ → ♊ 2:26 am

Color of the day: Orange
Incense of the day: Frankincense

Achieving Your Goals

Did you set some goals that you wanted to achieve this year and haven't completed?

First, write down what you wanted to achieve, what you did achieve, and what has yet to be completed. Take your time; there may be other goals you set since the beginning of the year. You want to work on earlier goals.

Assess if the goal is worth completing. Situations change. Opportunities sometimes are not what they seem, and we can find we bit off more than we can chew.

List the three most important goals to finish. Write them down. Place upon your altar, and also on your bathroom mirror, your refrigerator, and your work desk.

Every day do one thing to complete your goal. Ask your gods for guidance to complete your paths. You will be surprised what you can finish when you set your mind to the tasks.

Boudica

September 15

Monday

3rd ♊

Fourth Quarter 10:05 pm

☽ v/c 10:05 pm

Color of the day: Ivory

Incense of the day: Lily

honor Aging

In Japan, Keiro no Hi is the national holiday to honor the longest-living people in society. Today, honor your own aging process. Stand in front of the mirror, fully naked. Look at your body from head to toe, smiling. Don't let any critical thoughts creep in. Keep your mindset positive and affirmative. Know that every change in your body is a page in the story of your life. You have earned those wrinkles and gray hairs. You have earned the scars and lumps. Run your hands lovingly over your face and body, saying:

Like the seasons ever changing,
my body is rearranging,

I love this life and welcome aging,
my spirit is rearranging,

I bless the changes and don't fight time,

I love this temple, this body of mine.
  Dallas Jennifer Cobb

 September 16

Tuesday

4th ♊

☽ → ♋ 11:24 am

Color of the day: Maroon

Incense of the day: Geranium

Let the Outside In

As long as the day is beautiful, open up every window in your home for at least a few hours, and work this magical spell to get the energy moving and blow out the spiritual cobwebs. Using lavender oil or a lavender infusion, start with the window closest to your front door and work your way around the house clockwise. Open each window and trace a pentagram on the window frame with your lavender, stating:

Open, open, blow in the breeze,

Blow out the cobwebs, I ask you please.

Let in the clean air and let out the stale,

Fresh air and fresh thoughts to my mind avail.

If you have flowers blooming in your garden, cut some and bring them in. Allow Mother Nature to become part of your home today and the fall air to cleanse away stagnant energy before you have to close things up for the winter.

  Mickie Mueller

September 17
Wednesday

4th ♋

Color of the day: White
Incense of the day: Lavender

Legend of the Maneki Neko

The story of Maneki Neko and his good fortune dates back to the 1600s, when a prosperous businessman took refuge from a downpour under a tree. Across from the tree was a small, impoverished temple, tended by a priest who shared his meager meals with the temple cat, Tama. As the businessman stood there under the tree, he noticed the cat across from him, beckoning with his paw. Intrigued, the businessman left his shelter to go better check out the cat. No sooner had he crossed the path than a bolt of lightning struck the tree under which he had just been standing. The man then befriended both the priest and the cat. As a result, they never went hungry again and the temple became prosperous. Upon his death, Tama was buried in the temple's cat cemetery with great honor, and the Maneki Neko, or Beckoning Cat, was created. It is believed that good fortune will befall households or businesses that display a Maneki Neko.

Laurel Reufner

September 18
Thursday

4th ♋

☽ v/c 2:38 pm
☽ → ♌ 11:10 pm

Color of the day: Green
Incense of the day: Nutmeg

hail, hail, the Gang's All here

Thursday is a day good for group pursuits. With Mabon just a couple days away, this is a great time to plan some type of group project. In many parts of the United States, homeless shelters are getting ready to open. Food banks start major drives for blankets, coats, and scarves to prepare for the coming cold months. Some charities look for people to go to the homes of elderly people to cover their windows in plastic to help prevent cold drafts from coming through.

Get your group together and decide what to do. Then gather in a circle, hold hands, and recite the following:

We come together, hand in hand,

And vow to help our fellow man.

Work together in trust and love,

And praise our deities up above.

Kerri Connor

September 19
Friday

4ḥ ♌

Color of the day: Rose
Incense of the day: Thyme

Theater of the Play of Magic

Create a simple, bare, and open altar. Breathe, ground, center, and align. Gather up life force to cleanse and consecrate the altar to your magical work. This altar is your Theatre of the Play of Magic. Whenever you choose to consciously place an item or symbol upon this altar, it will instantly recognize this as an affirmed act of magic and will respond as such. Be very aware of what you place on this spell altar, as it will come into being.

To seal this spell and align with this altar as your Theatre of the Play of Magic, repeat the following while raising power:

I am an actor in a play,

A play that happens every day.

This altar is my theater blessed,

And on it are placed in what I am dressed.

Release the power into the altar and declare the work done.

Gede Parma

 ## September 20
Saturday

4ḥ ♌

Color of the day: Brown
Incense of the day: Rue

Gathering in the harvest

As the magical world gears up for Mabon, the main harvest, it is time to look to what we're harvesting on the inner planes. Have we achieved all we had hoped to achieve when we planted this year's "seeds" either at Imbolc or Ostara? If not, why not? As we harvest our gardens in preparation for the great feast, we can contemplate all of those things, and decide, without judgment, what we can do better in the future.

Gather some colorful leaves to decorate the harvest table with, and in doing so, allow yourself to go trancy. If a leaf you've gathered is too dry, send energy toward letting go of one unachieved goal, with love and respect toward yourself. Then crumble the leaf and watch the breeze take it. With the more supple leaves, think about the goals you've accomplished, and say to yourself:

I am filling my life with color and abundance.

Keep these leaves for your altar, and be at peace.

Thuri Calafia

September 21
Sunday

4th ♌

☽ v/c 12:33 am

☽ → ♍ 11:54 am

Color of the day: Gold
Incense of the day: Eucalyptus

UN International Day of Peace

Peace Spell

Today is Peace Day, the International Day of Peace established by the United Nations in 1981. It is a day for meaningful activities for peace, and a perfect day for a peace spell.

Purchase blue helium balloons.

Take a bowl of fresh spring water, and add lavender oil or fresh lavender buds. Insert your athame or hand into it, saying:

I consecrate this water to peace.
May peace flow from it.

Using the consecrated water and a brush, paint the peace sign on each balloon while chanting the Great Invocation of Peace Day:

May peace prevail on Earth.

Give each balloon to a friend or stranger, so that they may bring peace into their homes. Or take the balloons to an outdoor space, and release them to spread peace far and wide.

Other Peace Day activities can include a minute of silence at noon, or making origami peace doves.

Deborah Lipp

NOTES:

September 22
Monday

4th ♍

☉ → ♎ 10:29 pm

Color of the day: Lavender
Incense of the day: Rosemary

Mabon – Fall Equinox

A Mabon Ritual

Mabon honors the dual nature of life and death—darkness and light. It is a sabbat that combines sadness and celebration. We mourn the passing of the Great Son (Mabon), but also celebrate the bounty of the harvest. Just as nature enters the season of rest, Mabon returns to Mother Earth for regeneration and eventual rebirth.

To honor this sabbat, place one white and one black candle on your altar. In the center, place one red apple to represent Avalon, the Land of Apples where some traditions believe Mabon was held captive. As a symbol of rebirth, also have on hand a small bowl of spring-flowering bulbs, which are available now. Light the candles and say:

You walk the paths of darkness and light,

You do not fear the coming of the night.

Again you'll rise from the mists of Avalon,

For you are Mabon, the Great Son.

As a lasting tribute to this holiday, plant the bulbs. When they bloom in the spring, you'll remember Mabon and the cycle of birth, death, and rebirth.

James Kambos

NOTES:

September 23
Tuesday

4th ♍

☽ v/c 8:15 am

☽ → ♎ 11:59 pm

Color of the day: Gray
Incense of the day: Ginger

Celebrate Bisexuality Day

Those who number themselves among the bisexual population of the world still often feel marginalized and misunderstood, not only by many in the straight community, but also in some ways by the LGBT community.

That's why Celebrate Bisexuality Day (today!) is a great opportunity to magically lend your support to the beautifully inclusive bisexual community. Light one pink and one purple candle. Place your right hand over your heart, and direct your left palm out as if taking an oath. Say:

Just as I lovingly celebrate bisexuality, may all beings on earth lovingly celebrate bisexuality. May all feel free to love whom they wish. May every being treasure, and revel in, their own sexuality. May everyone love and respect one another completely, now and always.

In your mind's eye, see the candlelight as the light of love and acceptance, and envision it spreading to the hearts of all beings on earth.

Tess Whitehurst

NOTES:

September 24

Wednesday

4th ♎

New Moon in ♎ 2:14 am

Color of the day: Yellow
Incense of the day: Honeysuckle

Autumn Fairy Spell

The new moon is a great time for looking inward. This quiet spell welcomes in the nature spirits of autumn as you to ponder the mysteries of the changing seasons.

Fill your tub with warm water and Epsom salt, and light some fall-colored candles. Float several chrysanthemum blossoms into the tub; use different shades of green, purple, orange, yellow, and brown. As you soak in the tub, call upon the fairies of the changing trees and the autumn blossoms:

Sprites of changing seasons, teach me

To face life's changes gracefully.

Beauty that comes in many forms

Remains as lovely as it transforms.

Dear fairy folk, I embrace your wisdom

As I watch the changing of the seasons.

Feel the beauty of the earth around you. As you've invited in the fairies of the autumn, listen to their messages of the power of life and the deep lessons of what real beauty is—not the magazine pictures, but the true inner beauty of strength, wisdom, and the grace of yourself as a spiritual being.

Once you have truly heard the messages of the autumn Fae, and you're ready, say:

Thank you, spirits of the Fae,
as you return to your realms,
harming none along the way.

Be sure to leave a bit of bread and honey outside as an offering later on.

Mickie Mueller

Notes:

September 25
Thursday

1st ♎

Color of the day: White
Incense of the day: Clove

Rosh hashanah

Mother Earth's healing Charm

Since autumn is when many of the energies of the plants withdraw back into the earth, as She prepares for the rest that winter brings, I like to concentrate more on using stones and roots in magic rather than leaves and flowers.

This charm is a very simple healing charm designed to lend healing energy to you through harvest time. To make this charm, all you need is to find a smooth white stone outside somewhere, then wash it in cold water and light a light-blue candle. Go into a meditation holding the stone, and visualize light-blue energy streaming down into your third eye and through you, into the stone. When you feel the stone is fully energized, chant:

Forged in the earth, smooth white stone,

Filled with power to heal and mend.

Ancient magic to flesh and bone,

Healing force you now lend.

Carry the stone with you.

Michael Furie

September 26
Friday

1st ♎

☽ v/c 8:39 am

☽ → ♏ 10:29 am

Color of the day: Pink
Incense of the day: Cypress

An Apple Blessing

Today is Johnny Appleseed Day. It commemorates the work of John Chapman, a nurseryman who traveled west, planting apple trees and selling saplings to other settlers along the way. Although he worshipped in the Christian way, he also showed great reverence for nature in his actions. So he is a popular historical figure among Pagans as well.

Celebrate this holiday by doing something with apples. Decorate with images of fruit, trees, and Johnny Appleseed himself. You might visit an orchard to pick apples, hold a potluck feast with apple-smoked pork and apple pie, or plant an apple tree in your yard. Here is a blessing for you to use:

Apple trees are sacred,

As everyone must know.

We remember Johnny

Wherever apples grow.

So we say a blessing,

Wherever they may be:

Blessing on the apples

And blessing on each tree.

Elizabeth Barrette

Notes:

September 27
Saturday

1st ♏

Color of the day: Indigo
Incense of the day: Pine

Petition Yemaya for Protection

In many Santerian traditions, Saturday is the day of the orisha Yemaya. Her sacred number is seven, thus it is no coincidence that she is honored on the seventh day of the week. Yemaya, queen of the sea, is considered the mother of all orishas and is a mother figure for all her devotees. She is also a protectress of practitioners of the occult.

Take time today as a magickal practitioner to set out a tray of offerings to Mother Yemaya, to honor and thank her, as well as to ask for her continued protection over you and your loved ones. Her colors are blue, white, and crystal clear. Traditional offerings include white and blue candles, white roses, watermelons, plantains, cowrie shells, and seven silver-colored coins.

Blake Octavian Blair

September 28
Sunday

1st ♏

☽ v/c 4:31 pm

☽ → ♐ 6:50 pm

Color of the day: Amber
Incense of the day: Almond

Worth One's Salt

That salt is such a valuable product is shown by the myriad expressions and folklore than surround it. If we "take something with a grain of salt," we remain skeptical, harkening to ancient healing traditions where a small bit of salt was added to medicaments in hopes it would enhance the response. In medieval times, salt was stored in a vessel called a "Salt," and feast participants were seated "above the salt" or "below the salt," depending on their status. Likewise, to be "worth one's salt" was to be worth one's salary and refers to times when soldiers or workers were paid with salt or its equivalent.

To us magickal folks, salt is a sacred substance used for protection, psychic protection, grounding, cleansing, and purification. Keep a tiny bowl of salt in your sanctum; use a pinch here and there as needed, and remember to be "worth your salt."

Susan Pesznecker

September 29

Monday

1st ♐

☽ v/c 11:29 pm

Color of the day: Gray
Incense of the day: Hyssop

National Coffee Day

Coffee! That magickal, mystical, stimulating, delicious elixir so many of us cannot do without every morning. There is more to the growing, manufacture, distribution, preparation, and consuming of coffee than can be written here.

Coffee drinkers, sit quietly over your first cup of the morning or last cup of the day and reflect on all that coffee gives you: a lift, a boost, a calm spot of rest and pampering in the midst of a busy day. For those who do not partake of it, add whole coffee beans to a mojo bag created to awaken your creativity or heighten your divination powers. Say:

From the earth,

Blessed by water, wind, and sun,

All appreciation and gratitude

For every step of the process

That brings this beverage to me.

Emyme

September 30

Tuesday

1st ♐

Color of the day: White
Incense of the day: Basil

Touchstone

Today is Saint Jerome's Day, celebrated by the Pueblo people. Saint Jerome was a priest, linguist, hermit, translator, Bible scholar, and hospice administrator.

Today, celebrate the many roles you play. I'm a daughter, sister, partner, mother, librarian, teacher, volunteer, author, and friend, to name a few. How about you? Find five small stones, four similar and one distinct. Lay the four stones in four directions, and the other in the middle.

Touch the western stone:

Sturdy earth, great mother, guide me,

Touch the north stone:

Air, bless me with inspiration,

Touch the east stone:

Fan the fire of decisive action,

Touch the south stone:

Water, nurture all I do,

Pick up the center stone:

Touchstone, spirit, be with me,
and be all of these, in every role.

Carry the touchstone with you.

Dallas Jennifer Cobb

October

"Halloweeeen, the witches riding high … Have you seeeen their shadows in the sky?" So begins a rhyme I learned as a grade school student. Halloween then was October's crown, a magical time of mystery and excitement—and a time to fill a pillowcase with candy bars in an hours-long orgy of trick-or-treating. The magic of Halloween and Samhain is still with me; my love for the month of October grows stronger with each passing year. October is all about preparation—and change. The weather dampens, temperatures drop, days shorten, leaves fall, and everything ebbs as Earth slips inexorably toward winter's deep sleep. But even as Earth's energies seem to chill and settle, there remains much to do. It's time for wintering-in: to dress warm and light a fire on the hearth. Time to brew pots of tea and sink deep into books and study. Time to launch plans that will blossom in the spring. Magical tools begun during autumn and finished during winter and early spring will be heavy with accumulated power and intention. Divination studied throughout these months will tap deep into your psyche, leaving you with skills previously unimagined. Embrace the lessons of dark, wise October.

Susan Pesznecker

October 1
Wednesday

1st ♐

☽ → ♑ 12:41 am

Second Quarter 3:33 pm

Color of the day: Topaz
Incense of the day: Bay laurel

Take Back Your Power

Sometimes we give our power away because at the time it seems easier than rocking the boat. Sometimes shock, injury, or sorrow can chip away at the bright, shining pieces of your spirit, but that power belongs to you, so take it back.

Burn some rose incense while doing this meditation. Lie down someplace comfortable with a quartz crystal on your heart chakra, and visualize little stars that used to be part of you scattered to the wind. Now feel the crystal ignite and pulse with your own being. It becomes a beacon, sending out wave after wave of a signal that attracts these "soul pieces" that belong to you. Feel them coming back to you as if they're following the signal home. One by one you feel these stars returning to your body until they have all returned and you glow with your personal power.

Mickie Mueller

October 2
Thursday

2nd ♑

☽ v/c 12:18 pm

Color of the day: Crimson
Incense of the day: Apricot

Gandhi Jayanti

Today is Gandhi Jayanti, the birthday of Mahatma Gandhi. It is celebrated in India with prayer, ceremony, art, singing, and, for devotees of Gandhi, refraining from meat and alcohol. It was declared the International Day of Non-Violence by the United Nations in 2007.

Meditate on peace. Imagine a problem that you have. Now imagine that there is a nonviolent, peaceful solution—you don't have to know what the solution is, just imagine that it exists. Hold the clear image of that feeling in your mind.

You're going to create art about your problem, of whatever type suits you: painting, sculpture, collage—anything. Gather your materials and focus on nonviolent solutions. Send the feeling of a peaceful solution into your materials, so that everything you use becomes a magical tool.

Place your finished work of art on your altar, knowing it is working with you toward a peaceful solution to your problem.

Deborah Lipp

ʻOctober 3

Friday

2nd ♑

☽ → ♒ 4:00 am

Color of the day: Purple
Incense of the day: Violet

Love My home

Nothing is more important than having a home where you can go at the end of the day and feel peaceful, secure, and loved. While it isn't always possible to have the perfect retreat, you can help to make your home perfect for you.

First, make sure all your doors and windows have secure locks. It is always good to check your windows and doors a couple times a year to make sure they are in good working order. Locking windows will also keep air conditioning inside during the summer and heat in during the winter.

Use aromatherapy to make your home smell familiar and fresh. Rose quartz brings calm and warmth to the home. Finally, place in your home things that speak to you. Fill your home with memories, reminders of good times and things that make you feel warm all over.

Boudica

October 4
Saturday

2nd ♒

☽ v/c 2:32 pm

Color of the day: Black
Incense of the day: Ivy

Yom Kippur

Releasing Guilt

In honor of Yom Kippur, the day of atonement, engage in a day-long practice to release guilt and to help yourself feel spiritually clear, light, and free. Wear something simple, with natural fibers and light colors. Instead of fasting, perhaps choose to eat mostly whole plant foods (such as fruits, veggies, nuts, grains, and beans) and to drink only water, juice, and tea.

Before sunset, record in your journal any things you still feel guilty about, perhaps under the heading "Guilt Inventory." Then hold the inventory in your open palms and say:

Great Goddess, I release these things to you. Please lift the guilt from my heart and transmute any negative effects of these things into positivity and healing, in all directions of time. Thank you.

Safely burn the paper in a fireplace or cauldron. Then shower or bathe and finish by smudging yourself with white sage or palo santo.

Tess Whitehurst

October 5
Sunday

2nd ♒

☽ → ♓ 5:24 am

Color of the day: Orange
Incense of the day: Hyacinth

I Am Ready for a Relationship

There comes a time after much healing, restoration, reconciliation, growth, and deepening when we are each ready to embark on a new journey, in a new relationship, with a new person.

This spell is to send that call out into the universe to bring the right person to you at the right time.

Consider the qualities you would like in a prospective partner or lover, and project these qualities as energy signatures into a beautiful piece of rose quartz.

Set the rose quartz under the moon as it waxes, and when the moon is full, pray to the Moon Goddess for this lover to come.

Gede Parma

October 6

Monday

2nd ♓

☽ v/c 3:38 pm

Color of the day: White
Incense of the day: Clary sage

Poppet Fertility Magic

For this spell, you'll need to make a small poppet, or magic doll. It needs to be big enough for you to easily stuff, but that's the only size requirement. You'll also want to either draw on facial features with permanent markers or embroider them. Name the doll. (This will be either your name or the name of a friend who has asked for a little extra help.) Stuff the doll with a mixture of sunflower seeds and either dried ginger or mint. In the tummy area, place a small rose quartz. Sew the doll shut.

Place the doll on an altar between green and red candles, calling on whichever fertility deities you choose. Allow the candles to burn for a half hour daily for as long as you feel is needed.

Laurel Reufner

NOTES:

·October 7

Tuesday

2nd ♓

☽ → ♈ 6:07 am

Color of the day: Scarlet
Incense of the day: Bayberry

Star Scrying

Past the autumnal equinox, the nights grow longer. Trees shed their leaves and stand bare against the brilliant sky. The veil between worlds is slowly thinning. Now is a good time for scrying.

For this spell, you need a black bowl and enough water to fill it. Rainwater is best, but tap water will suffice. Go to a safe, quiet place outside after dark, somewhere that you can see the stars. Fill the bowl with water and set it to reflect the sky. Gaze into it and say:

> Bowl of water,
>
> Colored black,
>
> Catch the sky and
>
> Send it back.
>
> Ancient starlight,
>
> Silver rays,
>
> Show me past and
>
> Future days.

Search the glittering ripples for glimpses of what has been or what could be.

Elizabeth Barrette

·October 8

Wednesday

2nd ♈

Full Moon in ♈ 6:51 am

☽ v/c 10:20 am

Color of the day: Brown
Incense of the day: Honeysuckle

Lunar Eclipse

Change, Change, Change

In October, we see many changes around us, such as leaves changing colors, then falling, and temperatures also falling. Other changes may be going on behind the scenes as well. Are new people coming into your life? Are old friends scarce? It is a time when things die off, to make room for the new.

While change may be difficult, it can lay the framework for a strong, new future. Under the full moon, say these words:

> The changes all around me
>
> Don't have to be good or bad.
>
> They simply are to prepare me
>
> For the future to be had.

Take some time to meditate under the full moon, and say goodbye to those things in your life that are leaving.

Kerri Connor

October 9
Thursday

3rd ♈

☽ → ♉ 7:44 am

Color of the day: Turquoise
Incense of the day: Balsam

Sukkot begins

Throw Away the Key Spell

Grief can paralyze us and prevent us from living. When you feel you're ready to move on, try this spell; you are the only one who can set yourself free from pain and sorrow.

You'll need the Five of Cups card from the tarot, as many candles as you wish in cheery colors, an old key you don't need, and a glass of sweet red wine. Put the card in the reversed position on your altar, and light the candles. Hold the key above the flames; in your imagination, see the key turning in a lock and opening a door. Then say:

No more sorrow, no more grief.

I hold the key to set myself free.

Sip the wine—allow yourself to taste the sweetness of life again. On a sunny autumn day, throw the key into a body of running water. Hold your head high and walk away.

James Kambos

October 10
Friday

3rd ♉

☽ v/c 8:49 pm

Color of the day: Pink
Incense of the day: Alder

Pulse Point

Place your pointer and middle fingers over the pulse point just below your thumb. Move them gently until you feel your pulse. Now pause, becoming aware of it. This movement, this rushing of food and oxygen through your body, this never-ceasing work done day in and day out, second in and second out, for every day of your life—this is your lifeblood you're feeling, and it's yours alone. Use this as a point of meditation. Sit quietly, feeling your pulse. Close your eyes and be aware of the pulsing life force surging through you. Envision the blood rushing through your veins and arteries, a perfect gift of ongoing life and energy. The vessels themselves represent earth, the oxygen they carry is part of air, the life-giving heart provides the life-spark fire, and the blood is your own water of life. Remove your fingers, breathe deeply, and be thankful.

Susan Pesznecker

October 11

Saturday

3rd ☿

☽ → ♊ 11:51 am

Color of the day: Blue
Incense of the day: Magnolia

Meditrinalia Festival

S cholars occasionally disagree on the origin or even the existence of some of the more obscure Roman goddesses and gods. However, it is wise and honorable to accept even the least of myths.

The goddess Meditrina is purported to be a goddess of health, longevity, and wine. On this day, the new wine was introduced. Some of it was mixed with the last (dregs) of the old wine and kept for medicinal purposes. Gather like-minded enophiles for a wine tasting this evening. Introduce a variety of wines that are new to you, always in moderation. Provide juices and grapes to those who do not drink alcohol and to the designated drivers. Offer toasts to health and longevity. At the end of the evening, pour a small amount of wine into the earth as an offering to Meditrina.

Emyme

 October 12

Sunday

3rd ♊

Color of the day: Gold
Incense of the day: Juniper

A hearth Blessing with Brigid

M any people associate Sunday's solar energies with the masculine divine. However, Sunday is also a day sacred to a goddess with solar ties, the Celtic Brigid. Brigid's associations with the sun as well as the hearth fire make today a perfect day to work with this goddess to bless your hearth and home. Place a tealight candle in a holder upon your home's hearth (fireplace mantle, kitchen stove, or family altar). Then recite the following:

Brigid of the hearth and home,

Brigid of the solar flame,

*Bless our home with your light,
inspiration, and healing.*

With this hearth flame, we honor you.

So mote it be!

Light the candle and envision the light radiating from its flame growing larger and larger until it illuminates your entire home in a golden bubble of light. Allow the candle to safely burn itself out where you can watch it. Blessed be.

Blake Octavian Blair

·October 13
Monday

3rd ♊

☽ v/c 1:58 pm

☽ → ♋ 7:30 pm

Color of the day: Silver
Incense of the day: Narcissus

Columbus Day (observed)

To Rid Oneself of harm

This spell should be cast during a waning moon. It is designed to cleanse you of any astral and spiritual imbalances and any psychic harm sent your way.

Take a cleansing bath in salted water. If desired, this spell can be cast while still in the bath. Close your eyes, relax, and go into a meditation. Visualize yourself breathing in brilliant white light flecked with gold. See this light cleansing your spirit and strengthening your aura. When you feel strong and ready, chant this spell:

Drive away all harm this night.

Dissolve discomfort, unrest, dis-ease.

Golden power, shining light,

Through your magic, I am freed.

If you have cast this spell in a cleansing bath, drain the tub and rinse yourself off with pure water from the shower to wash away any psychic residue.

Michael Furie

NOTES:

October 14

Tuesday

3rd ♋

Color of the day: Gray
Incense of the day: Cedar

Unplugging Ritual

Make the entire day today a ritual of self-care. With Mercury in retrograde, not a lot of spellwork can be accomplished, and computers will be buggy. So why not take the day off and just follow your instincts? Unplug your phone, turn off your cell. Get off those social media sites and take a day off to reconnect with yourself without an electronic device stuck to your brain. Go "camping" in your own home by unplugging whatever you can. We should do so anyway, with many devices, when they're not in use, as they use energy even while off.

Tell your friends and family you're not available, and then, do whatever your heart desires. Take a long bath, do artwork, or read a book. Take a long walk somewhere particularly special or beautiful, light candles … honor and celebrate you! As you go to sleep tonight, thank your gods and yourself for how special and wonderful you are.

Thuri Calafia

 October 15

Wednesday

3rd ♋

Fourth Quarter 3:12 pm
☽ v/c 7:27 pm

Color of the day: Yellow
Incense of the day: Lilac

Sukkot ends

Sacrifice for harvest Day

In Rome, the rite of the October Horse was celebrated today. A chariot race was held after which the right-hand horse of the winning team was slaughtered, and its blood used to bless the Forum, and farmers' fields. The sacrifice of the strongest beast was meant to produce a good harvest.

Today, skip the animal sacrifice, but make an offering in favor of good harvest, no matter where you live. Make dinner, setting aside a plate of what you ate. Pour a glass of what you drank—wine works well. At dusk, stand barefoot on the earth, looking west into the sunset. West is the direction of autumn, the earth, and the color red.

Pour drink on the earth:

I offer the blood of good spirit.

Place food on the ground.

I offer sustenance in thanks and praise.

Place your hands on the ground:

*I give thanks, abundant earth,
for this harvest.*

Stand, opening your arms wide:

Bless the farmers' fields.

Dallas Jennifer Cobb

NOTES:

October 16
Thursday

4th ♋

☽ → ♌ 6:29 am

Color of the day: White
Incense of the day: Jasmine

Sink Negative Thoughts

Here's a use for those old lead fishing weights. Don't use them for fishing—they're toxic to wildlife, but useful for a bit of magic!

Lead can silence negative thoughts in your mind that hold you back, and banish them for good. Take a black string about a foot long; I like embroidery floss. Then take two lead fishing weights, and tie one on each end of the string. Now, whatever negative thoughts cross your mind, say them out loud one by one. As you say each thought, tie a knot in the string. The knots trap your words, and the lead on each end of the string silences them.

When you've finished, put the knotted cord in a dark-colored bottle until those thoughts are long forgotten. At a later date, burn the knotted cord and reuse the lead weights to repeat this spell whenever you wish.

Mickie Mueller

ʘ October 17
Friday

♃ ♌

Color of the day: Rose
Incense of the day: Orchid

Attract Friendship

We all want to attract the attention of someone special into our lives, but we sometimes overlook the best kind of someone special. There is a saying that a true friend thinks you're a good egg, even when you are half-cracked.

I recommend "friendship candles" to help you focus, preferably a three-day one. Anoint the candle with honey and rosewater. Work the spell with the intent to find your best friend. Do not consider love, romance, or any special attribute in your spell, but rather just someone you can be yourself with.

At the end of three days, it is time to socialize. You are *not* going to find your BFF sitting at home. Pick a likely spot—social events, next-door neighbors, meet-ups, or anyplace where you will find people like yourself. Don't push it; it will come on its own and will be a relationship for life.

Boudica

♥ October 18
Saturday

♃ ♌

☽ v/c 9:10 am
☽ → ♍ 7:08 pm

Color of the day: Brown
Incense of the day: Patchouli

Self-Love

This is a portable self-esteem spell. Use the waning moon to banish negativity while bringing good feelings. Self-love helps attract the love of others.

Gather these ingredients: water, lavender essential oil, rose petals, and a lemon.

Concentrate on driving away your negative feelings. See the colors and textures of anxiety and pain replaced by colors and textures of happiness. Say:

I bless this work with self-love.

Put four cups of water into a pot. Add twelve drops of lavender essential oil, saying:

I banish anxiety. I bring peace.

Add twelve rose petals, saying:

I banish pain. I bring love.

Add the juice of a fresh lemon, saying:

I banish negativity. I bring happiness.

Pour energy into the mixture, saying:

Darkness is banished and light comes to me. So mote it be.

Boil for twenty minutes. Strain.

Carry a spray mister with you. When you feel the need, spray yourself with portable self-love. Keep the remaining mixture refrigerated. Replenish as needed.

Deborah Lipp

NOTES:

⊕ **October 19**

Sunday

4th ♍

Color of the day: Amber
Incense of the day: Almond

A Spiritual Unveiling

As we move closer to Samhain, the veil continually thins. Every day this month can be used for spiritual communication; you do not have to wait for Samhain to arrive.

Do your spirit guides or ancestors have messages for you? If you are new to communing with spirits, try using a pendulum, asking yes-or-no questions. Before you begin a session, burn a little frankincense. Then say the following:

Spirit guides, I call to you.

Ancestors, I call to you.

Friends and family, both known, and unknown, I call to you.

From across the veil, I call to you and invite you to commune.

Join your essence with mine

In the presence of the Divine.

In the beginning, keep your sessions short. Spirit communication can be exhausting work, but when it helps you to unveil a spiritual truth, it is well worth it.

Kerri Connor

October 20

Monday

4th ♍

☽ v/c 11:30 pm

Color of the day: Lavender
Incense of the day: Lily

Deep Emotional Detox Bath

Draw a warm bath. Dissolve into it one cup sea salt, a half cup Epsom salt, and a quarter cup baking soda. Crush the leaves of seven sprigs of fresh rosemary between your fingers as you strew them across the surface of the water. Add the petals from three fresh white roses. Near the water, place a white candle and a stick of frankincense incense, and light.

Stand over the water and direct your palms toward it. Relax your body and mind and then visualize bright white light streaming down through the top of your head, down to your heart, and out through your palms into the water as you say:

Yemaya, Great Goddess, may this
water purify me deeply, inside and out.
On every level, and in all directions
of time, may I be purified and healed.
Thank you.

Soak for at least forty minutes. Keep drinking water on hand and drink generously.

Tess Whitehurst

October 21

Tuesday

4th ♍

☽ → ♎ 7:12 am

Color of the day: Black
Incense of the day: Ylang-ylang

Attract Good Luck Spell

One of the most popular tokens of autumn, Indian corn is a very good spell ingredient to use for attracting prosperity, protection, or general good luck. This spell helps attract and keep good luck.

You'll need one ear of Indian corn with the husk, yellow or light-blue yarn, and a piece of yellow or orange fabric. For a moment, handle the corn. Look at its colors, and silently give thanks to the indigenous people of the Americas who developed corn, the mother of all grains.

Next, fold the husk down over the corn, and begin to wrap the yarn around the husk. As you wrap the yarn, feel good luck being drawn to you. Keep wrapping the yarn as you speak this charm:

Seed of all seeds,

Giver of life,

Bring me all I will need.

Tie the ends of the yarn together, and wrap the corn in the fabric.

James Kambos

·October 22

Wednesday

4th ♎

Color of the day: Topaz
Incense of the day: Lavender

A Compost Spell

At the end of the growing season,
garden plants are pulled up or
cut down. The earth is tilled under
for the winter.

Now is a good time to apply
compost, giving it time to break
down prior to spring planting. You
can spread the compost pile from the
garden, gathered during summer.
You can buy compost. In autumn,
it's actually acceptable to spread fresh
manure. In fact, that often costs less
than finished compost, and it will
decompose enough to be safe by the
time planting season rolls around.

Most magic is aimed at growth,
but compost magic focuses instead
on decay, as a part of the natural
cycle. As you spread the compost,
recite this charm to help it work:

All that dies

Comes apart, breaks down,

Loses self,

Turns from green to brown,

Goes to earth,

Becomes dirt and food,

Lies in wait

For spring's new green brood.

                    Elizabeth Barrette

NOTES:

October 23

Thursday

4th ♎

☉ → ♏ 7:57 am

☽ v/c 1:22 pm

☽ → ♏ 5:10 pm

New Moon in ♏ 5:57 pm

Color of the day: Purple

Incense of the day: Mulberry

Solar Eclipse

Money habits Tarot Spell

Use this spell to get your spending habits under control. You'll need the Ace of Pentacles, the Emperor, and the Six of Wands from a tarot deck. You'll also need a red and white candle, plus a smooth piece of obsidian that fits comfortably in your hand. Place the candles on your altar, with the Emperor card between them. The Ace of Pentacles goes to the left, and the Six of Wands to the right. Set the obsidian just below the Emperor card. Draw on the promise of wealth and prosperity promised by the ace card, and see the victory over your spending that's suggested by the Wands. Call upon the will of the Emperor card and the assistance of the universe to help you think before shelling out your hard-earned cash. Afterward, carry the obsidian with you as a reminder of your promise to yourself.

Laurel Reufner

October 24

Friday

1st ♏

Color of the day: Coral

Incense of the day: Rose

Debt Repayment

Does someone owe you money? This spell brings payment on a past-due debt.

Using play money or a check, place the amount owed to you in the center of your altar, saying:

Money, money, come back to me.

Take black tea and create a circle around the money, starting in the east and going clockwise, repeating the words of the spell as you do.

Light a green candle at each quarter, starting at the east, saying the words of the spell.

When you return to the east, say:

Money, money, you have come back to me!

Let the candles burn all the way out.

Leave a pinch of the tea on the doorstep of the person who owes you money. Or mail a friendly note reminding the person of the debt. Include the pinch of tea in the envelope.

Keep the money on your altar until the debt is repaid.

Deborah Lipp

October 25

Saturday

1st ♏

☽ v/c 12:11 pm

Color of the day: Gray
Incense of the day: Sage

Buildup to Samhain

One week to go before we celebrate Samhain. Many choose this time of year to do seasonal house cleaning. Make the windows sparkle, drive the dust from the corners, change the linens, and unpack the festive fall decorations. Now is a perfect time to cleanse your home with this easy ritual.

Open every window of the house. Light a cone or stick of sage incense, or a sage votive candle, in a container you can safely carry. Walk into every room of your home; pause with one step in and raise the container slightly, saying:

Out with stale and in with fresh,

This sage my home will cleanse and bless.

The next few months bring holidays high,

Bring all my loved ones safely nigh.

Emyme

·October 26

Sunday

1st ♏

☽ → ♐ 12:40 am

Color of the day: Yellow
Incense of the day: Marigold

Seal Your Thresholds

The time when spirits roam the land is upon us, and while you may want to honor them in upcoming rituals, you can choose to keep uninvited random spirit energies from crossing your threshold and lingering. Let's shore up those thresholds so that only the invited may cross.

Mix together salt, rosemary, and cinnamon in a pot full of water, and allow it to boil. When the mixture cools, put it in a spray bottle and mist it across every threshold in your house, plus the doors and windows. Then light a white candle in the heart of your home to activate the barriers:

I seal the thresholds in my home

Against all spirits uninvited.

As I do state by flesh and bone,

They'll pass me by and not feel slighted.

The only spirits may cross my door,

The ones that I shall choose.

The rest shall find another floor

To rest their ghostly shoes.

Mickie Mueller

NOTES:

October 27
Monday

1st ♐

☽ v/c 12:18 pm

Color of the day: Ivory
Incense of the day: Neroli

Light a Lamp for Diwali

Today is the Indian festival of Diwali, known as the festival of lights. Although which deities and stories are celebrated varies from region to region and family to family, the common theme is that of illumination of good over evil, and awareness of one's inner light. Celebrants also commonly ask the goddess Lakshmi for her blessings of prosperity and abundance upon their family for the coming year.

To celebrate, clay oil lamps called diyas are lit by the dozens and even hundreds. In honor of your own personal triumphs and inner light, gather several tealight candles and light them on your altar. Then light your favorite meditation incense. As the candles burn, meditate on your triumphs of the past year and express your wishes for the coming year. Chant the following mantra to invoke the blessings of Lakshmi:

Om shree Mahalakshmi namah!

May your inner light illuminate your path! Namaste.

Blake Octavian Blair

October 28
Tuesday

1st ♐

☽ → ♑ 6:03 am

Color of the day: Red
Incense of the day: Cinnamon

The Power of "No"

Sometimes a single word can change our lives. Today, remember the famous "no" uttered by Prime Minister Metaxas of Greece, forbidding the creation of Italian military bases there. It sided Greece against the Italians and Germans, and with the Allies throughout World War II.

In school and at work, we are often forced to accept things we want to refuse. As children we are taught to comply. But as adults we need to cultivate the power of "no." Learn how to politely refuse to do things that go against your beliefs and values. Learn to stand up to pushy people and bullies, and side against racism and sexism. Know when to say no.

Identify one area in your life where you need to limit your involvement. And today, use the power of "no," combined with good manners, to politely decline further involvement.

Dallas Jennifer Cobb

October 29
Wednesday

1st ♑

☽ v/c 11:01 pm

Color of the day: Brown
Incense of the day: Marjoram

Going Quiet: A Day of Silence

Embracing silence is a test of will for many of us, but it can be a deeply spiritual experience that links us to our pre-industrial-technical roots.

Plan a day of silence, welcoming silence both inside and out. This means not speaking (unless an emergency absolutely requires it) and not communicating through text message, social media, etc. It also means immersing yourself in silence—turning off television, laptop, MP3 player, phone, etc.

Spend your day in silence, and instead of listening to the din of people and media, listen to yourself. Work with meditation or divination. Read. Take a long walk. Listen actively to wind and rain and birdsong. Be especially aware of what you hear that is new, unexpected, or usually obscured by other noise. Journal regularly throughout the day, reflecting on the richness of the experience.

Susan Pesznecker

 October 30
Thursday

1st ♑

☽ → ♒ 9:52 am

Second Quarter 10:48 pm

Color of the day: Green
Incense of the day: Carnation

The Mask of the Unified Self

Get a premade mask from a craft shop, and place it on your altar. Hang a mirror above your altar at eye level. Using black or deep blue candles, cast and call in your usual way, and ask your deities for help in seeing yourself truly, as you are now as well as who you can become. Holding the mask, allow yourself to go trancy, and then look yourself in the eyes in the mirror.

Chant:

Lords and ladies and guardians,
from around, below, and above,

As I seek and find the truth within,
let me see with eyes of love.

Let yourself ride the waves of trance. The object here is trance, so if the chanting falls off, it's fine. As you deepen, open yourself to the pictures and symbols you see, noting whether you are seeing a particular place on the mask they belong to. Let yourself drift.

Immediately after, make a sketch of your mask as you saw it, and then paint the mask, either inside or outside of circle.

Thuri Calafia

NOTES:

October 31
Friday

2nd ♒

Color of the day: White
Incense of the day: Vanilla

Samhain – halloween

Opening Your Third Eye

The third eye is the pineal gland located near the center of the brain, in the middle of the forehead. This gland is affected by light, and stimulation of the pineal is believed to increase psychic ability. Samhain is the ideal time to open this eye and peer into the unknown.

Sit in a chair and lean your head back. Take a small polished amethyst or sodalite stone, and place it on your third eye. Close your eyes. Visualize a beam of pure white light pouring down, through the stone, into your third eye, filling it with power. When you feel full of energy, say these words to seal the spell:

Power of light, power of second sight,

Pour into me on this holy night.

Mighty Goddess, winter's Crone,

Open my eye to that unknown.

All forms of divination and scrying are improved by this magic.

Michael Furie

November

November may appear to be a brown and dreary month, depending on one's particular climate, but it holds a quiet beauty. While in our mundane lives we're often preoccupied with planning for the upcoming winter holidays, this time of year, as fall begins to fully embrace winter, offers opportunities to observe wildlife, stargaze, and see aspects of nature that are sometimes overlooked. Observe the beauty of leafless trees; see their true form and shape. Look at fallen leaves, often etched with frost, and watch for trees bearing winter berries and cones. Walking through the woods in November can be eye-opening. Without the thick growth of underbrush and biting insects, we can see a bareness of Earth seldom revealed. Work magic with the season's first snowfall, or save some snow for a future ritual. In addition, collect leaves, twigs, and nuts to make a wreath. Have a bonfire celebration; work fire-magic. Think of November as a special time of waiting, an interlude between the vibrant fall and the coming winter. This is a time of darkening days, but also a time for indoor work or, if weather permits, outdoor magic. Welcome the wonder of transition.

Ember Grant

November 1
Saturday

2nd ♒

☽ v/c 2:22 am

☽ → ♓ 12:37 pm

Color of the day: Blue
Incense of the day: Sandalwood

All Saints' Day

New Friends

Yesterday you probably honored the departed. Today, bring new people into your life with this spell to draw friendship.

Create a circle in your most welcoming room. At east, south, west, and north, place sweet pea and/or passion flower, and an unlit pink candle.

Ground and center.

Beginning with east, light the candle and say:

*Brightness draws new friends to me
from the east.*

Repeat at each direction, and then pause silently at the east before going to the center.

Seated in the center, imagine that the circle of light you're in is a beacon, drawing friends to you. That light will remain a part of your home even after the candles go out. Drum, sing, dance, or tone to send energy into the light and into its attraction.

Allow the candles to burn out. Carry a bit of the sweet pea/passion flower with you at all times.

Deborah Lipp

NOTES:

November 2

Sunday

2nd ♓

Color of the day: Orange

Incense of the day: Heliotrope

Daylight Saving Time ends at 2:00 am

All Souls Day

So many (one might say all) Christian church holidays are borrowed or adapted from Pagan celebrations.

In the Catholic Church, this is All Souls Day. On this day the church honors the departed with a special mass. The names of those who have passed are written on slips of paper, and the papers are placed in a basket or container and blessed by the priest.

Perform your own adaptation. Write the names of your dearly departed on brightly colored pieces of paper or index cards, and place in a glass bowl. Set the bowl on your altar with votive candles: blue for autumn and gold for Sunday. Meditate on those you honor. Concentrate on all the positive aspects of their lives. If possible, allow the candles to burn down completely.

Emyme

 November 3

Monday

2nd ♓

☽ v/c 4:05 am

☽ → ♈ 1:53 pm

Color of the day: Ivory

Incense of the day: Rosemary

Destroy a Curse Spell

If you think an enemy is working against you or you've had a run of bad luck, this spell will snuff out all dark energy that's directed at you. The spell ingredients you'll need are one black votive candle, a heatproof dish, sand, a brown paper lunch bag, and twine. Set the candle on the heatproof dish and light it. Let it burn a while until the wax begins to drip—feel any dark energy around you begin to weaken. Begin to sprinkle the sand on the candle until the flame goes out. As you sprinkle the sand, say:

By my own hand, I snuff out all dark energy.

By my own hand, I've set myself free.

Powers of the dark,

I hereby extinguish your spark.

Let the candle and sand sit undisturbed overnight. The next day, place the candle and sand in the bag, then tie it shut and bury it.

James Kambos

November 4
Tuesday

2nd ♈

Color of the day: Maroon
Incense of the day: Geranium

Election Day (general)

Job Improvement Knot Magic

Seek out a better job either in your current field or a field in which you long to work. Before beginning, you'll need to sit and brainstorm which qualities, skills, and talents you can bring to your chosen job. Next you will need 9 to 13 inches of either embroidery floss or hemp in yellow (confidence), green (money), and orange (vitality and adaptability).

Making sure your list is nearby, prepare to start. Light a candle in each of the same three colors. Ground and center yourself. Now, using your list, begin knotting the cord, with one knot for each item on your list. Begin by stating the first item on your list and tying a knot toward one end of the cord. Continue down the list, adding a knot to your cord with each item. Make each statement positive while visualizing yourself in your dream position.

Laurel Reufner

 ## November 5
Wednesday

2nd ♈

☽ v/c 8:25 am
☽ → ♉ 4:33 pm

Color of the day: Topaz
Incense of the day: Lilac

Choose a New Direction

If there were ever a day to choose a new direction and plant the seeds for its most ideal unfolding, today is it. So what do you choose? Would you like to move to a new home? Perhaps you desire a new love relationship, or a fresh chapter in a love relationship you're already in. Maybe a new job or degree is on the horizon, or the launch of a new business.

Brainstorm about your desire in detail. Explore it with some form of art: dance it, write it, paint it, or collage it. Begin to bring it from the watery realm of dreams into the earthy world of form. Once it begins to coalesce in your mind and heart, hold an agate to your heart with both hands. Channel the image and feeling of your manifested desire into the stone. Say:

Success, success, success.

Bury the agate near the base of a tree.

Tess Whitehurst

November 6
Thursday

2nd ♉

Full Moon in ♉ 5:23 pm

Color of the day: White
Incense of the day: Nutmeg

holy Moon Water

The full moon is a wonderful time for charging things with a burst of lunar energy. It is also the perfect occasion to create a simple holy water for use in spells, bless-ings, and ritual.

Start by filling a bottle, bowl, or other vessel with purified water. Add any crystals or herbs whose energy you wish to imbue your water with. A nice all-purpose combination would be moonstone with a handful of crushed white sage and a dash or sprig of rosemary. Place the vessel somewhere that it can bask in the moonlight overnight, perhaps on a windowsill, on a porch, or in your yard. Then recite a simple blessing like the following:

Lady of the Moon, shining bright,

Lend your lunar blessing this night.

Your silvery illumination

Blessing this holy creation.

Blessed be!

Retrieve your blessed holy water in the morning and use as guided.

Blake Octavian Blair

November 7
Friday

3rd ♉

☽ v/c 11:17 am

☽ → ♊ 8:45 pm

Color of the day: Purple

Incense of the day: Orchid

Unicorn Sight

Unicorns are mythical beasts resembling a horse or goat with a single horn. They represent the element of spirit, and they are forces of purity (which is more about the spirit than the body) and good. According to legend, unicorns can sense whether a person is honest or deceitful, treacherous or trustworthy.

For this spell, you need a small white candle and a figurine of a unicorn. Place them on your altar, and concentrate on enhancing your mystical perceptions. As you light the candle, say:

Form of white, horn of light,

Share with me your inner sight.

Cracked or whole, chalk or coal,

Lend me vision of the soul.

Let the candle burn out while you meditate on spiritual insight. Keep the unicorn in a safe place. Later, when you need to gauge someone's intentions, think of the unicorn and then trust your instincts.

Elizabeth Barrette

November 8
Saturday

3rd ♊

Color of the day: Black

Incense of the day: Rue

Longing for Connection

Are you longing for an intimate spiritual connection? Are you missing or lacking that sense of community with like-spirited people? Here is a spell to open your life to empowering spirit connections with others.

For this spell, you will be praying to Grandmother Weaver, the matrix of all.

Sit in darkness with an unlit candle before you, the color of which embodies the kind of connection you are looking to forge. Breathe, ground, center, and align. Sink down into the Great Abyss and become conscious of Consciousness. This is the Weaver beholding her Mystery. It is here you will find your heart. A shining piece of the Great Web of the Infinite comes out of your heart; perhaps there are many. Focus on each one and travel down these strands of the Wyrd. Open to their possibilities for you.

Light the candle and sit in stillness, heart open and willing.

Gede Parma

November 9
Sunday

3rd ♊

☽ v/c 11:22 am

Color of the day: Yellow
Incense of the day: Eucalyptus

Clean the house for the holidays

You will probably be having friends and relatives visiting your home over the holiday season, so you want to make your home as warm and inviting as you can.

Sweep your house; use pine cleaner wherever you can use it safely, for cleaning and grounding. Follow up with a good rinse using a seasonal scent (apples, cinnamon, pumpkin spice, pine, etc.) to give a warm and homey smell to the house. Keep some on hand to refresh your home over the season.

While I love pine and pumpkins at this time of year, remember that stones also add to the feel of the house. Smoky quartz at the door repels unwanted guests. Rose quartz and watermelon tourmaline radiate warmth and attract friendship and love. Scatter the stones about the house to give a flow to the feeling. Colors of the season always add visual appeal and set the focus for your holidays.

Boudica

NOTES:

November 10
Monday

3rd ♊

☽ → ♋ 3:38 am

Color of the day: Silver
Incense of the day: Lily

Blessing with Water:
Sacred Waters

Enrich your magickal practices by collecting and creating sacred waters. A jar of spring water left out overnight to charge under a full moon carries lunar energies and is wonderful for spells involving mystery, divination, and love. Charging water under the light of celestial bodies (planets, stars, comets) likewise infuses the water with those attributes. Water that charges throughout the day under the full summer sun is useful for magickal workings of growth, strength, power, and passion. Capture special waters for unique purposes: the first rain, the first snowfall, rain from melted icicles or hail, condensed dew, or water from river, ocean, or other bodies of water.

Use your sacred waters to clean and consecrate tools, to sip or sprinkle during ritual, for brewing infusions, or for any other magickal purpose. (Note: Only drink wild water if fully certain it is safe to do so.)

Susan Pesznecker

November 11
Tuesday

3rd ♋

Color of the day: Scarlet
Incense of the day: Cinnamon

Veterans Day

Spell to Banish Jealousy

Take some time to write down, on scraps of paper, all the things you feel jealous about. Name names, as well as the ways in which you feel jealous or envious of others. Throw each of these jealous "thoughts" onto a large green (preferably a sickly green) cotton cloth, until you have a big pile. Then tie the corners together with cotton string, making a bundle. Allow yourself to become as sickly green and angry as the cloth bundle you're holding, projecting all the anger and sour feelings you can muster into the bundle.

When you feel ready, throw the bundle into a fire and watch it burn. Say:

As this bundle of jealous thoughts burns, so do the feelings and emotions burn away in me.

Now, inscribe a light blue or pink pillar candle with all the things you genuinely love and value about yourself. Whenever you feel jealous, look at and light the candle, remembering you are just as awesome as anyone else.

Thuri Calafia

NOTES:

 November 12

Wednesday

3rd ♋

☽ v/c 4:16 am

☽ → ♌ 1:44 pm

Color of the day: White
Incense of the day: Bay laurel

A Flexible Mind

Do you have a flexible mind? Is your mind open and receptive, or are you closed-minded and reluctant to change? Do you willingly consider new ideas, or do you hold fast to your own die-hard beliefs?

Having strong beliefs is one thing—it's good to be able to stand up for what you believe in and to be confident that your beliefs and choices are good ones. However, if you never put yourself in the position to explore other beliefs and ideas, especially ones counter to your own, then you can never be completely secure in your own beliefs as they stand, because you haven't bothered to evaluate the alternatives. It's like claiming vanilla ice cream is the best without ever having tried a single taste of chocolate.

Meditate on how you need to open your mind. Where can you let it bend a little to let in new ideas?

Kerri Connor

November 13

Thursday

3rd ♌

Color of the day: Turquoise
Incense of the day: Clove

Knot Magic for Pain

To help relieve pain from injuries or help ease chronic pain, knot magic is useful. Obtain red cord of a natural fiber, such as cotton, as this will help the cord draw out the pain. Rub the cord on the afflicted area, then tie a knot on one end of the cord. Chant this spell:

I draw the pain into this knot.

Relief from pain is hereby sought.

As the cord burns, the pain is released,

Wellness restored and suffering ceased.

Rub the cord on the afflicted area again, and tie a knot on the other end of the cord. Chant the spell again. Rub the cord on the afflicted area one last time, and tie a knot in the middle of the cord. Chant the spell again.

Press the cord to the afflicted area, and with all your willpower, send the pain into the cord. Finally, burn the cord safely. Bury the remains.

Michael Furie

 November 14

Friday

3rd ♌

Fourth Quarter 10:16 am

☽ v/c 9:53 pm

Color of the day: Rose
Incense of the day: Alder

Banish a Difficult Person

The ethical way to banish a bad person from your life is to bless them with goodness … far away from you!

Meditate on the best possible place for this person.

Ground and center.

Consecrate a piece of writing paper by touching it to each of the four elements, saying:

*I consecrate this paper to luck
and good fortune.*

Consecrate a pen the same way. You'll use this pen only for magic from now on.

Write a letter to the person, saying something like this:

I am so happy for you. I'm glad you found your dream job and that your life is doing so great in [place]. It's great the move has worked out so well and that you are so happy. I wish you the very best of luck in [place]. May all good things continue to come to you.

Mail the letter to Person's Name, General Delivery, Place You Selected.

Deborah Lipp

November 15

Saturday

4th ♌

☽ → ♍ 2:08 am

Color of the day: Indigo
Incense of the day: Ivy

Put It in Perspective

S o things didn't go your way. Someone unfriended you on Facebook or gave you a rude gesture on the highway. It seems like it should be just a little thing, but sometimes harsh criticism digs away at your peace of mind like that little hangnail until it's all you can think about. Time to stop picking at it and do something!

You don't need a thicker skin, you just need to put things in perspective. Light a white candle and concentrate on the flame. Say out loud at least ten positive things that have been said about you by others. Now think about that one thing that's bugging you, and tie three knots in a black string. Now say:

This really doesn't matter.

Then light the string in the candle flame and drop it into a fireproof dish. Make sure you burn it all up. Breathe deeply, knowing that you've released it.

Mickie Mueller

NOTES:

November 16

Sunday

4th ♍

Color of the day: Gold
Incense of the day: Frankincense

Art, Education, and Culture

Surround yourself with books, beauty, song, and dance today in celebration of Saint Margaret, patroness of Scotland. Married to the rough and uncouth King Malcolm, Margaret became known for the civilizing influence she brought to the king and to Scotland. Named patroness of arts, culture, and education, she reminds us how these can help us to find happiness and success.

Today, carve out time for the appreciation of art and culture, and invoke her spirit. Visit a gallery or art show, take in a play or movie, or loll in bed with a good book. Invite a friend to attend an event with you, and then spend time talking about what you loved about it. Or go alone to a gallery and sit quietly observing the beauty and brilliance of famous artists. Be inspired and invigorated by art and culture—be uplifted, informed, and educated. Celebrate civilized beauty, art, education, and culture.

Dallas Jennifer Cobb

November 17

Monday

4th ♍

☽ v/c 6:11 am
☽ → ♎ 2:30 pm

Color of the day: Lavender
Incense of the day: Clary sage

Baking for Love

Today is National Homemade Bread Day. It's a time to celebrate one of the basic skills of home and hearth. When you cook from scratch, you take care of yourself and the people you love. Bread is the food of life, sacred in many Pagan traditions. It lends itself well to spellcraft in the kitchen.

For this spell, you need to make a loaf of bread. Once the dough is in the loaf pan, decorate the top with a magical symbol, either cut with a knife or painted with melted butter. Runes, ogham, elemental signs, etc., will all work; choose whatever represents your goal. As you put the bread in the oven, say:

Mixing the dough,

Kneading it out,

Speaking of love,

Without a doubt,

Watching it rise,

Baking the bread,

Magic's afoot

And spell is said.

The spell is activated when the bread is eaten.

Elizabeth Barrette

NOTES:

 November 18

Tuesday

4th ♎

Color of the day: Black
Incense of the day: Bayberry

Fit Like a King

Many of us, including myself, could use a bit more exercise in our daily routine. A magickal boost and talismanic reminder couldn't hurt the process, right?

Print an image of the King of Pentacles tarot card and hang it in a place you will see it often. The suit of pentacles represents to many people not only monetary wealth but also the domain of physical health. The King, being at the end of the suit's progression, is at the top of his game, with a good handle on his health. Any time you pass the image, especially before exercising, place your hand on the image and visualize yourself meeting your exercise and health goals. Visualize yourself being as fit as the King!

Blake Octavian Blair

November 19

Wednesday

4th ♎

☽ v/c 9:25 am

Color of the day: Yellow
Incense of the day: Lavender

Garifuna Settlement Day

Today is the celebration of Garifuna Settlement Day in Belize, where the Obeah folk religion is prevalent. Like many of the religions from the African continent, the history of Obeah is murky. Misunderstandings and distrust often arise from unfamiliar beliefs. However, that very uncertainty also opens up many possibilities. Those who honor all religions as valid can find the good and positive in any faith.

In the spirit of all good energy of Obeah, fashion a talisman or charm to draw out positive thoughts. Or you may wish to create a witch bottle or protection bag in the name of Obeah to banish the negative and protect your home.

Emyme

November 20

Thursday

4th ♎

☽ → ♏ 12:31 am

Color of the day: Purple
Incense of the day: Jasmine

Magical Foods

Nothing says holidays like good food. Food brings warmth and comfort to home, table, and friends.

Barley is a healing food and should be added to stews and soups. I recommend chicken soup with barley.

Apples are for love, and cinnamon is for healing; a good apple pie will always bring out the best in family relations.

Maple syrup is for money drawing as well as long life. A wonderful way to add to your family's well-being is to add maple syrup to corn bread and serve it with stews and soups.

Mint is used to attract money and offer protection for travelers. Say "good luck" and "safe travels" with a sprig of mint as part of a table decoration or on a gift.

Finally, after each party, sprinkle salt and then sweep to remove leftover energy so you can start anew with the next group gathering.

Boudica

November 21

Friday

4th ♏

Color of the day: White
Incense of the day: Mint

A Bread Spell

On this day in Greece, grains are honored. This ancient practice probably began as a ritual to thank the goddess Demeter. Dishes made of grains are prepared in most regions of Greece today, with each area having their own specialty.

This bread spell is appropriate for today. Prepare your favorite bread; it can be from scratch, a mix, or even a frozen loaf of bread. Before baking, brush the shape of a pentagram on the bread using milk. When done, bless the bread. Slice a piece for each family member, and eat mindfully as you think of how grains sustain us.

End by slicing a piece for your home. Tear this slice into four pieces. Place each piece outside your home in all four corners of your property. This way you'll share your thanks and good fortune with the birds and the earth.

James Kambos

NOTES:

November 22
Saturday

4th ♏

☽ v/c 12:53 am

☉ → ♐ 4:38 am

☽ → ♐ 7:19 am

New Moon in ♐ 7:32 am

Color of the day: Gray
Incense of the day: Magnolia

Saint Cecelia Obstacle Removal

Today is the feast day of Saint Cecelia. She's invoked to clear paths and remove obstacles, and she's especially fond of artists. All magical practitioners are artists who work with symbols, colors, and chants to embody and channel divine energy and beauty. So Saint Cecelia can help clear away anything that may be holding you back from experiencing your art, and life in general, to the fullest.

Create or obtain a jar candle depicting Saint Cecelia, and light. Also light a bundle of dried sagebrush or desert sage and smudge your aura as you chant:

> Saint Cecelia, I call on you. Thank you for clearing all channels and opening all paths to my ideal life experience. Thank you for blessing my life with a feeling of harmony, contentment, ease, and flow. Blessed be.

Extinguish the sage, and allow the candle to burn all the way down. (Extinguish/relight as necessary.)

Tess Whitehurst

NOTES:

November 23

Sunday

1st ♐

☽ v/c 10:16 pm

Color of the day: Orange
Incense of the day: Juniper

Shoot for the Stars Spell

With this barely formed crescent, this tiny sliver of a Diana's bow moon tonight, we are called upon to dare to dream big, to shoot for the stars! Take a silver candle and a gold coin, and ponder these words from the Charge of the Goddess: "Keep pure your highest ideal. Strive ever toward it; let nothing stop you or turn you aside."

What is your highest ideal? In a perfect world, what would be your vocation, your honor, your best of all possible ways of being? Project that energy into your candle, saying:

As I pursue my own highest nature,
all else will come—
in its own time.

Breathe deeply, knowing that what you have planned for yourself in this life is coming to pass, and that you are, indeed, on the right path, that in this, you will prosper. Light the candle, letting some of the silver wax drip onto the gold-colored coin, to be kept as a reminder.

Thuri Calafia

 November 24

Monday

1st ♐

☽ → ♑ 11:31 am

Color of the day: White
Incense of the day: Hyssop

Spell to Make a Decision

If you are faced with a decision and need some way to make a choice, you can use a crystal pendulum for help. Hold the pendulum in your strong hand over two cards on which you have written each choice. The card over which the pendulum swings in a clockwise circle bears the correct decision for you. Hold the pendulum in both hands and pray this spell to the Goddess:

Indecision plagues me now,

Magic crystal guide my way.

Sunwise circle, you will show

On which path I should stay.

When you feel ready, hold the pendulum over each card, noting its swing. If the pendulum swings clockwise over both cards, it indicates that both choices are equally valid and safe for you. If it swings counterclockwise or any other way over both, it indicates that neither choice is in your best interest and you should look at other options.

Michael Furie

November 25

Tuesday

1st ♑

Color of the day: Gray
Incense of the day: Ginger

Safe and Sound home

While most of us don't have to hunt and gather food to last until spring, many of us have learned that Mother Nature can have a temper. She can send storms of a vicious nature that cause power to be out for days or weeks, or snow that can literally bury a house until the people inside find a way to dig out.

Being prepared in these situations can be the difference between life and death. Make sure your home is stocked with enough batteries, nonperishable foods, firewood, shovels, bottled water, flashlights, and blankets to last a few weeks. It's always better to be overprepared. Once you are ready physically, then prepare magically. Walk around the outside of your home sprinkling black salt. As you scatter it, say:

Protect my home,

My family too.

Grant us safety

To see us through.

Kerri Connor

 November 26

Wednesday

1st ♑

☽ v/c 10:30 am

☽ → ♒ 2:23 pm

Color of the day: Brown
Incense of the day: Marjoram

A Travel Charm

While most of us view travel as a time of excitement and wonder, even simple or accustomed trips may carry a twinge of anxiety. Have I forgotten something? Am I safe? Will I find my way?

Before you leave home, take along a pebble or twig from your front yard, and keep this as a place-anchor, a token to help direct your safe return. As you board airplane, bus, train, or car, place your hand on the vehicle's surface and pause for a moment, then repeat this charm:

Fleet of foot and swift of wing,

Safe in your arms this charm I bring.

As you depart the vehicle, place your hand on it again and murmur a thank you. Once you arrive home, bury the pebble or twig in your front yard as a permanent place-anchor. Settling your hand on the door to your home, offer thanks, and as you step over the threshold, feel the warm protection of your own home.

Susan Pesznecker

November 27

Thursday

1st ♒

Color of the day: Crimson
Incense of the day: Balsam

Thanksgiving Day

Giving Thanks

Today in the United States, it is Thanksgiving Day. This celebration has a convoluted and complicated history, but its simple desire to give thanks for abundance, family, endurance, and love is both beautiful and deeply needed in our world today.

Here is a spell to empower every day to be a day of giving thanks.

Say aloud this affirmation:

Each day I will arise and give thanks,

Each night I will lay down and give thanks.

In every act and every choice I give thanks,

I am a being of thanksgiving.

Gede Parma

 November 28

Friday

1st ♒

☽ v/c 12:14 pm
☽ → ♓ 5:03 pm

Color of the day: Pink
Incense of the day: Violet

Ma'at's Goodness

Ancient Egyptians used today to honor the goodness of Ma'at, goddess of truth and balance. It was against the feather of Ma'at that the hearts of the deceased were judged. Decorate a small wreath to hang in your home that will welcome in the goodness of Ma'at, encouraging balance and trust among loved ones. Wrap a feather boa around a small foam or straw wreath form. Add some flowers or greenery for decoration, including a couple of ostrich feathers, which are representative of Ma'at.

Place the wreath on your altar before a blue candle, and light some sandalwood or a similar incense. I've provided an invocation, but feel free to create your own.

Heavenly Ma'at, bestow your goodness on this home.

From the chaos of life, bring balance and truth to this home and to those who dwell within.

So may it be.

Laurel Reufner

November 29

Saturday

1st ♓

⧫Second Quarter 5:06 am

Color of the day: Blue
Incense of the day: Pine

Protection from Psychic Vampires

Historically in Romania, today is a day to ward off vampires. We are all affected by psychic vampires—people who take without giving, who suck energy out of everyone around them, or who carelessly refuse to recycle good energy back out into the world.

Traditionally used to repel vampires, garlic is a powerful tool. Historically garlic was rubbed around door and window frames, hung over the main door of a house, and hung in braids in the kitchen. In crisis situations, garlic necklaces were worn for protection.

Become aware of the psychic vampires in your realm. Think of them while you make garlic-rich foods, like roasted garlic spread on crusty bread, garlic soup, or hummus with extra garlic. Eat these with gusto. Like the farmer who discovered that feeding garlic to his cows kept the flies off of them, consciously ingest the intention of ridding yourself of psychic vampires everywhere.

Dallas Jennifer Cobb

November 30

Sunday

2nd ♓

☽ v/c 3:47 pm

☽ → ♈ 8:14 pm

Color of the day: Amber
Incense of the day: Hyacinth

Banish Stress

Think about your stress. What's weighing on your shoulders? Now begin to rub your hands together, and as you do, allow all of the stress that you've been holding on to to be drawn down into your hands as they rub together. Then take a sheet of bubble wrap, and hold one bubble between your fingers. Think of something that caused you stress recently. Send that stress into the bubble, focus, then pop it. Felt good, didn't it? Do it again.

One by one, send your stress into the bubble wrap and pop it, dissipating the stress. Feel the stress leaving your body through your fingertips as you pop away. Go ahead and pop every bubble, then take a deep cleansing breath in through your nose and out through your mouth. Put the bubble wrap in a brown paper bag and throw it away in your outside trash or recyling.

Mickie Mueller

December is a wonder-FULL month! Bright sunlight on glistening snow that fills us with magical wonder can turn into a blizzard, or to slushy, slippery roads that make our hearts leap into our throats! Yet we embrace this month of extreme changes. The solstice will arrive, and we will renew the cycle of contemplation and new expectations. For many Pagans, this "winding down" of the old year encourages us to finish things we started and get our affairs in order. We look to the promise of the sun's returning, of days getting longer, and new possibilities hovering on the horizon. We celebrate this renewal by getting together with family and friends and sharing our optimism for the coming year. Sometimes the magic of December gets lost in a flurry of shopping, planning, and parties that have little to do with our religious beliefs, but we can't ignore the special feelings that pervade the spirit of the season during this magical month. It is the time of year that most strongly calls to us to remember our past and celebrate our future in tune with the cycles of nature. It can be harsh, but more often December nurtures our inner child to explore and embrace the hope and possibilities of life ahead of us.

Paniteowl

December 1

Monday

2nd ♈

Color of the day: Gray
Incense of the day: Narcissus

Powers of Seduction and Sensuality

Water is an element that can invoke and evoke the most sensuous and seductive forces within and without.

Ground, center, and align. Sit in still meditation as you hold a glass of fresh water before you in your hands. Begin to raise the life force and channel it into the water, and let your imagination run wild with the full flourishing of your own powers of seduction and sensuality. Go for it! This gift is yours to yourself! When you feel the peak of power, drink in the water.

It is done!

Gede Parma

 December 2

Tuesday

2nd ♈

☽ v/c 9:42 pm

Color of the day: Maroon
Incense of the day: Basil

Holiday Diet Spell

The temptation to overeat is everywhere this month. Follow this spell to help you maintain your desired weight.

First, draw a figure of your body the way you want to look. Trace your finger over the sketch several times. Put the drawing away. If you leave it out, you may begin to obsess.

When you eat, hold the vision of your sketch in your mind. When eating at a holiday buffet, put a small portion of each food on your plate—and sit away from the buffet table as you eat. Enjoying holiday sweets is okay, but do this: Put a couple cookies or sweets on a pretty plate. Prepare a cup of tea or coffee. Enjoy your treat while sitting in a favorite easy chair. Savor the moment. Don't set unrealistic goals for yourself, and think of the image you drew earlier as you eat. You'll be fine.

James Kambos

December 3
Wednesday

2nd ♈

☽ → ♉ 12:15 am

Color of the day: Brown
Incense of the day: Honeysuckle

Tea Time for Prosperity

There is an old cliché saying, "You are what you eat." So the magickal mindset would naturally extend to metaphysical properties of the ingredients of the foods that we ingest as well. We all would enjoy a bit of extra prosperity (especially in the holiday season), and bergamot, one of the herbs associated with Wednesdays, has a prosperous vibration. Steep yourself a nice cup of Earl Grey tea, as bergamot is a featured ingredient in this classic blend. Stay with your tea as it steeps, and as the tea becomes darker and darker, visualize your prosperity growing more and more abundant. Repeat the following three times before drinking:

By rind of bergamot and leaf of tea,

May I grow abundant with prosperity.

With it harming none,

So mote it be!

Drink and enjoy your enchanted beverage.

Blake Octavian Blair

December 4
Thursday

2nd ♉

Color of the day: White
Incense of the day: Myrrh

National Cookie Day

Everyone has a favorite cookie, or keokje, and this is the time of year for cookie baking, according to numerous belief systems. The opportunities to celebrate this day can be as simple as buying slice-and-bake cookies from the supermarket, or as elaborate as taking several days to bake dozens of cookies for gifts.

Somewhere in between those two options is the cookie swap. Invite your coven or group for an informal gathering—the only clause being that each person must bring at least two-and-a-half dozen cookies and several seasonal bags or tins, and each person must leave with no less than two dozen cookies. Store-bought cookies are fine.

After the swap, bless the food and people with a short spell like the one below, and sample some of the "cakes" along with the "ale" of your choice.

Nourishment and cheer,

To all who gather here.

Emyme

December 5
Friday

2nd ☿

☽ v/c 1:45 am

☽ → ♊ 5:28 am

Color of the day: Coral
Incense of the day: Thyme

Drawing to Yourself

Friday is a good day to draw the universe to your doorstep. There are many spells that can be done using powders and foods to draw fortune to your doorstep—especially money spells.

Honey is a classic drawing item. It is used in love spells to "stick" two people together, and is kept on business altars to draw customers and business.

Money-drawing powder can be cornmeal and/or sugar, and is sprinkled on the ground outside a business to attract customers.

To draw money to yourself, carry a piece of malachite in your pocket, and for fast money, add a piece of cinnamon stick. Mistletoe at this time of year is not just for kissing; it also draws prosperity to the home.

Finally, an old favorite: a money-drawing sigil—$$¢¢$$—to place on business cards, invoices, and abundance checks.

Boudica

December 6
Saturday

2nd ♊

Full Moon in ♊ 7:27 am

Color of the day: Black
Incense of the day: Rue

A Spell for Restful Sleep

Winter brings long, cold nights. It is a time of rest. The wind stirs outside the walls. The full moon shines down on the smooth white snow so that the world is dark and bright all at once. This is a good time for invoking the moon's power over the realm of sleep.

To cast this spell, you need a silver coin, such as a dime or quarter. Hold the coin under the light of the full moon. Focus on your desire for peaceful sleep, then say:

Full moon, round and bright,

Clad in coat of white.

Through the sky you go,

Over ice and snow.

Silent watch you keep,

Guard me in my sleep.

When you're ready for bed, place the coin on or near the headboard and repeat the incantation. Think about the full moon keeping watch as you drift to sleep.

Elizabeth Barrette

December 7
Sunday

3rd ♊

☽ v/c 4:52 am

☽ → ♋ 12:34 pm

Color of the day: Gold

Incense of the day: Marigold

Charm for Nighttime Travel

If you have to travel at night, especially during "The Gloom" time from Samhain to Imbolg, it is a wise idea to recite a verbal charm of protection around yourself to keep any unpleasant beings at bay.

This charm invokes the power of the night itself to keep you safe, as if in a magical cocoon. Visualize yourself wearing a black hooded cloak of protection as you cast the spell:

Of all dangers, I am free,

In shroud of shadows, secure from harm.

Wrapped in darkness, safe and warm,

Cloak of night, protect me.

Michael Furie

December 8
Monday

3rd ♋

Color of the day: Silver

Incense of the day: Lily

Buddha Invocation

It's Bodhi Day, which celebrates the moment the Buddha cut through all doubt, ignorance, and illusion in order to realize enlightenment. In short, it honors the Buddha (which means "enlightened one") becoming the Buddha. Some people sit in meditation for days or even weeks to celebrate. Instead, set a timer for ten minutes. Sit comfortably with your spine straight, and take some deep breaths. Smile gently and close your eyes. Rest your open palms in your lap, facing upward. Notice your breath as it goes in and out. When a thought arises, don't fight it, just notice it. When your mind wanders from this calm attentiveness, bring it back. When the timer dings, place your left hand on your heart and your right hand over it. Say nine times:

Om mani padme hum.

Then say:

Siddhartha, Shakyamuni, I call on you. Please infuse my awareness with peace and my actions with love. Thank you.

Tess Whitehurst

December 9

Tuesday

3rd ♋

☽ v/c 7:14 pm

☽ → ♌ 10:14 pm

Color of the day: White
Incense of the day: Ylang-ylang

holiday Protection Spell

Feel a little safer during the holiday travel season with this simple and decorative charm. The end result is meant to be hung in your vehicle.

Take any combination of holly or mistletoe sprigs and cinnamon sticks. Tie them together into a little bundle with either red embroidery thread or narrow red ribbon. Charge the charm to keep away dangers while you travel, as well as to keep you and your loved ones safe while on the road. Hang from your rearview mirror or some other convenient spot in your car where it's presence won't be too distracting. If you do your holiday travel by some other means, take the charm materials and chop them into smaller bits, no bigger than an inch. Place them in a small cloth bag, and tuck it into your luggage.

Laurel Reufner

 December 10

Wednesday

3rd ♌

Color of the day: Yellow
Incense of the day: Lavender

Light of Liberty

The Goddess of Liberty—whom some equate with the Statue of Liberty—holds a torch that lights the way and shines upon you even in your darkest hour. During this dark half of the year, the reminder of a goddess bearing a torch to light the way can be comforting.

The short winter days and long winter nights can be taxing on people. A guiding light, a beacon, can help us make it through those days. As this goddess lights our path forward, she also lights a path to liberty, to freedom. The path to freedom is different for each of us. For some, freedom may simply be the feel of a warm spring sun of their face. For others, freedom may be what they find after meditating on inner issues all winter long.

Use this dark half of the year to meditate with the Goddess of Liberty to see what freedom she has in store for you.

Kerri Connor

December 11

Thursday

3rd ♌

Color of the day: Green
Incense of the day: Apricot

A Balance Spell

During the hustle and bustle of the holiday season, no matter which holidays we celebrate, it's easy to get caught up in trying to do too much.

Go to a local park, your own backyard, or a vacant lot where there is a tree with no lower branches. Approach the tree reverently, telling it in your mind that you are spent and you need recharging. Ask the tree politely if it will help you ground. Then send energetic "roots" down deep, right alongside the tree's roots. Lean in and touch or, better still, hug the tree. Allow it to take your fatigue and frustration. Breathe deeply and steadily, and just let those scattered energies go. As you inhale, smell the rich scents of the tree and earth around you, and let the steady, balanced energy of the tree fill you with vitality and wisdom. Honor yourself and your accomplishments, allowing rest when appropriate, knowing tomorrow is another day.

Thuri Calafia

 December 12

Friday

3rd ♌

☽ v/c 7:48 am

☽ → ♍ 10:19 am

Color of the day: Purple
Incense of the day: Yarrow

healthful hibernation

As the calendar rolls toward the longest night and shortest day of the month—the solstice—many people notice a decreased mood and energy level. Some may even feel full-blown depression, often called Seasonal Affective Disorder (SAD). Although SAD is often treated with light, new evidence now suggests the mood alterations are affected by our failure to mesh with cyclical, seasonal changes.

Make your own attempt at winter hibernation. Begin each day with a welcome to the sun. Eat seasonally: soups, stews, hot cider, roasts, and root vegetables. Turn the thermostat down, and don wool sweaters and fuzzy slippers. Keep the lights low after sundown, and engage in wintry activities: work on magickal tools, study divination, read, or plan the spring herb garden. At bedtime, turn out the lights and whisper blessings of gratitude for the nurturing comforts of winter and for the gift of light, which will soon return.

Susan Pesznecker

December 13

Saturday

3rd ♏

Color of the day: Gray
Incense of the day: Ivy

honor Thy Parents

The tradition of Saint Lucia's Day, celebrated in Sweden, is that the firstborn daughter wears pure white and a crown of candles, and serves her parents breakfast in bed. Today, let's all do a spell that honors our parents. Get pictures of your parents, together or apart. Set them on your altar. Regardless of your relationship with them, think about all the good things these people gave you, because cultivating gratitude for them is the highest honor. Even if you had a tough time with them, think about the strength and resilience you developed and how it has benefited you in life. Look at them lovingly. Take a deep breath, mustering as much gratitude as you can, and say:

For all you gave me, and all I received,

For all you taught me, and all I believed,

For all your love from which I was conceived,

Thank you, blessed be.

Dallas Jennifer Cobb

 December 14

Sunday

3rd ♏

Fourth Quarter 7:51 am

☽ v/c 9:11 pm

☽ → ♎ 11:05 pm

Color of the day: Amber
Incense of the day: Almond

Ice Fairy Incantation

The ice fairies painting on your windows and glittering in the trees are beautiful, but they are also the fairies that freeze your car door shut and leave a thin sheet of ice on your walkway. The ice fairies don't inconvenience you out of malice. They are merely the elemental spirits of winter doing what comes naturally and supporting nature in its wintery sleep.

This incantation can be spoken to honor the winter fairies and to invoke their protection as you travel into the weather:

Fairy friends, I'm sure of foot upon the ice,

As I admire your handiwork of beauty.

Fairy friends, I'm sure of tires as off I drive,

I honor thee, faeries of winter duty.

By winter flame, freezing water,
sleeping earth, and cold winds blow.

I shall be safe, I shall be sound upon
the ice and winter snow.

Mickie Mueller

NOTES:

 December 15

Monday

♄ ♎

Color of the day: Lavender
Incense of the day: Neroli

Spirits of the Season Spell

The holiday season can be tinged with sadness when we think of the loved ones who are no longer with us. But the spirit realm is active at this time of year, and our ancestors are eager to connect with us.

For this spell, you'll need these items: pine or a pine garland, old photos of your loved ones, and any old Christmas ornaments that have sentimental meaning. The pine will represent everlasting life, and the photos and ornaments will connect us with our ancestors.

For this ritual, it's best to use a fireplace mantle; if not, then use your altar, or a bowl that you can use as a holiday centerpiece. Arrange the pine, then place the photos among the branches. Here and there, place the ornaments as you think of the memories associated with them. Each evening, light a red candle to honor your ancestors as you meditate.

James Kambos

December 16

Tuesday

4℞ ♎

Color of the day: Red
Incense of the day: Cedar

Banish Unfairness

On the anniversary of the Boston Tea Party, which was a protest against "taxation without representation," use this spell to remove unfair treatment from your life.

You will need a white candle, lavender incense, saltwater, a balance scale, a picture of yourself, and some tea bags.

Pass the picture through the incense, saying:

By air, this picture is me.

Pass it over the candle, saying:

By fire, this picture is me.

Wet it with saltwater, saying:

By water and earth, this picture is me.

Place it on one side of the scale.

Pass each tea bag through the elements, naming the problem:

By (the element), this is (problem).

Then, place each on the other side of the scale. Watch it become more and more unbalanced.

Meditate on fairness, and send fairness energy to the scale.

Remove tea bags one at a time, saying:

This is more balanced.

Do this until the scale is balanced. Say:

So mote it be.

Deborah Lipp

NOTES:

December 17
Wednesday

4th ♎

☽ v/c 12:40 am

☽ → ♏ 9:52 am

Color of the day: White
Incense of the day: Marjoram

hanukkah begins

Multicultural Magic

Today is the first day of Hanukkah, the Jewish festival of lights. So many faiths practice the celebration of light at this time of year that the ritual feels almost universal.

Take time to illuminate your home, and celebrate the multicultural diversity that makes our communities bright, rich, varied, and textured. Use nine candles, the same number used in the Chanukiah, the nine-armed menorah used at Hanukkah. The number nine represents harmony, inspiration, and the perfection of ideas.

Use nine different candles. Place each one in a safe, fireproof holder. Create a safe and sacred space. Dim the lights. Look at each candle, meditating on someone you know from another culture. As you ritually light the candle, see their face bathed in light. When you have illuminated the candles, representing people from different cultural origins, sit bathed in light and know how much brighter life is made by their unique presence.

Dallas Jennifer Cobb

NOTES:

December 18

Thursday

4℞ ♏

Color of the day: Turquoise
Incense of the day: Nutmeg

To Loosen That Which Binds

You are bound. You are stuck. You feel lifeless and out of it. You yearn for freedom. You yearn for empowerment. You yearn for self-hood once more, in its splendor, in its deep soulfulness.

Ground. Center. Align. Feel into your being, and into its emana-tion, its auric radiance. Call upon your allies to circle round and hold space for you as you loosen the ties that bind.

Invoke strength from the earth and stars, and feel it crashing upon you, up through you, like waves of crystalline light, like fire of the earth. Feel all your bonds come free in this moment of sheer ecstasy. Let them go. Do not cling to them. You are free.

Stand and claim your sovereignty.

Gede Parma

December 19

Friday

4℞ ♏

☽ v/c 4:11 pm
☽ → ♐ 4:55 pm

Color of the day: Pink
Incense of the day: Vanilla

Spell of Detaching

Now, in the last sliver of the moon just before the sun returns, we are called upon to look at what attachments we still have that no longer serve us. The moon will be new on Yule this year, so tonight is a great time to let go, to detach from that which is no longer needed. For this simple spell, you first must write a list of unneeded attachments. Be honest with yourself about them; leave no stone unturned. Ask your-self if you really need to keep review-ing the hurts from this past year, if you honestly want the relationships that aren't working.

When your list is complete, twist the paper into a long bundle, and tie it with black cotton thread. Say:

> These attachments have twisted and
> thwarted my purpose. It's time to let
> them go.

Then save the bundle to be used to light the Yule fire two nights hence. Watch it blaze up with the energy of your passion, re-ignited! Be blessed.

Thuri Calafia

December 20

Saturday

4℞ ♐

Color of the day: Indigo
Incense of the day: Magnolia

Sadie, the Bargain–Shopping Goddess

Sadie, Sadie, Bargain-Shopping
Lady, what treasures can you
help me find?

Holiday shopping got you in
a panic? Need the perfect gift, an
unusual gadget, or just the right
something for someone special?

Look for Sadie! She is that short,
stout lady in the gray winter coat and
a purple scarf carrying shopping bags
filled to the top with treasures. Once
you spot her, follow her through
the store—she will lead you to the
priced-right bargain bins, close-out
racks, and in-store specials. Sadie will
lead you around the stores till you've
found the perfect gift for everyone on
your list.

Later at home, share an offering
of a glass of Irish cream and a foot
bath with the goddess of discount
shopping.

Boudica

 December 21

Sunday

4℞ ♐

☽ v/c 7:34 am
☉ → ♑ 6:03 pm
☽ → ♑ 8:25 pm
New Moon in ♑ 8:36 pm

Color of the day: Yellow
Incense of the day: Frankincense

Yule – Winter Solstice

Raven's Gift

A long time ago, Raven looked
down from the sky and saw that
the people of the world were living in
darkness. Raven wanted the ball of
light, which was hidden in sky-world
by a selfish chief. So Raven turned
itself into a spruce needle and floated
on the river where the chief's daughter came to drink. She drank the
spruce needle, became pregnant, and
gave birth to a boy, who was Raven
in disguise. The baby cried until the
chief gave him the ball of light to play
with. Then Raven turned back into
himself and carried the light high into
the sky. From then on, the people no
longer lived in darkness. Celebrate
Raven's gift today, on the solstice.
Turn off every light in your home.
Read Raven's story aloud, then turn
on lights and light candles until your
home fairly glows with brilliance.
Rejoice in Raven's gift!

Susan Pesznecker

December 22
Monday

1st ♑

☽ v/c 10:17 pm

Color of the day: Ivory
Incense of the day: Rosemary

A holiday Card Spell

The winter holiday season brings an annual surge in mail, both postal and electronic. People send a great many holiday cards to each other—but not all of the cards arrive safely. The mail slows down under the stress of extra traffic. Sometimes things get lost in transit.

This spell focuses on protecting holiday cards so they reach their intended recipients. You'll need a canceled postage stamp, preferably one with a holiday theme. Draw a pentacle over the stamp, charging it with these words:

Stamp and star,

Here you are,

Safely through the mail.

Let each card

Fly so hard,

Landing without fail.

Keep the stamp charm in the basket, tray, or other place you use to store mail. It will help your cards to arrive intact, coming and going.

Elizabeth Barrette

December 23
Tuesday

1st ♑

☽ → ♒ 9:52 pm

Color of the day: Black
Incense of the day: Cinnamon

Out with the Old, In with the New

Today is the Festival of Larentia, a goddess of the earth who commemorates the old year and celebrates the potential of the year to come. Spend the day cleaning out the old—not physical items, but simply clear your mind. Are there things that happened in the past year that you are still focusing on? Things that have not been resolved in the manner that you had hoped they would? Perhaps it is time to accept that they have indeed been resolved, just not to your satisfaction, and that you should move on. Sometimes we hold ourselves back while waiting for things to turn out the way we want them to.

Spend a few days meditating on these old issues and then release them. Learn what you need to from them, and then just let them go. A new year is coming. Give it the room it needs to grow and prosper.

Kerri Connor

December 24

Wednesday

1st ♒

Color of the day: Topaz
Incense of the day: Lilac

Christmas Eve

Love My Family Meditation

I'm sure I don't need to tell you that the holidays, even when going well, can be stressful. Today and tomorrow, many of you will be celebrating Christmas with non-Pagan family members. Or perhaps you're celebrating the end of Hanukkah with your family today.

Much as we love our families, they know how to get on our nerves the fastest way possible. Find a scented holiday candle that you find soothing. I would suggest one with a vanilla or a gentle evergreen scent. Find a spot in front of the lit candle where you can sit comfortably for a time. Now, watch the candle flame and try to calm your body. Take deep breaths, letting yourself enjoy the candle's soothing scent. Every so often, remind yourself that they are your family and you love them. It's just that sometimes you might not like them, and that's okay. However, you're not going to let your reaction to them ruin the holidays for you.

Laurel Reufner

 December 25

Thursday

1st ♒

☽ v/c 10:11 am
☽ → ♓ 11:07 pm

Color of the day: Crimson
Incense of the day: Mulberry

Christmas Day

Clementine Candle Spell

Clementines are popular this time of year, and it so happens that you can use one to make some really cool candle magic and impress everyone at your holiday gathering. Score the clementine around its center, and carefully pull the peel off in two pieces. One end has part of the pith sticking up from the peel—this is your wick. Pour olive oil into that half, exposing the tip of the wick. Place a penny over the wick to help it soak up oil, while saying under your breath:

Clementine, joy to find,
share good luck, yours,
theirs, and mine.

Carve a star-shaped hole into the center of the other peel. Then remove the penny, light the wick, and place the top on the candle. It will glow beautifully.

Let everyone know that eating one of the sections from the clementine candle will bring good luck throughout the year.

Mickie Mueller

December 26
Friday

1st ♓

Color of the day: White
Incense of the day: Mint

Kwanzaa begins

Self-Rejuvenation on Boxing Day

Today is Boxing Day. In the United Kingdom, it is tradition-ally the day when people box their gifts before heading home from holi-day travels. Others hold the day as a time to give gifts and money to the needy or those in service professions.

When celebrating the winter holidays at large family gatherings, the holidays can start to feel more like work than celebration. Dedicate today as a needed gift of rest for yourself (and your significant other if you have one). If you can't take a whole day to yourself, find an hour to set aside. Light a candle of a heal-ing color (purple and green are good choices). Visualize healing light from the candle surrounding you and rejuvenating the energy within your body and spirit. As the candle burns, engage in a relaxing, enjoyable activ-ity, such as reading, listening to music, knitting, or engaging in con-versation with your significant other.

Blake Octavian Blair

December 27
Saturday

1st ♓

☽ v/c 10:44 am

Color of the day: Brown
Incense of the day: Sandalwood

Cord Spell to Find a Lost Object

The crow is very good at finding things. Crows love to steal and collect shiny objects. If you need help finding something, invoke their keen observation and quick-witted-ness. You need a black cord with nine knots in it and a crow's feather. Poke the feather through a knot at the end of the cord, and lay the cord in a line across a table. Sit opposite the feather end of the cord, and light a white candle in the middle of the table. Slowly, pull the cord to you and chant:

What is lost I seek to find.

Knotted cord and feather of crow,

Let me now reclaim what is mine.

Reveal to me what must be known.

Once you have the feather in hand, snuff out the candle. Carry the cord with you as you search.

Michael Furie

December 28

Sunday

1st ♓

☽ → ♈ 1:35 am

Second Quarter 1:31 pm

Color of the day: Orange
Incense of the day: Juniper

Banish Bad Luck

Holy Innocents' Day (today) is a Christian observance memorializing Herod's slaughter of innocent children. It has been traditionally considered to have unlucky connotations. This—combined with today's other aspects—make it a great day to banish the "bad luck" of the previous year and to transmute negativity into blessings. Place a tall, white jar candle on a plate. Surround it with a circle of salt, and light. Also light some frankincense incense. Hold your fingertips together near your heart and, using a swishing motion, flick them outward nine times, as if you are flicking negativity away from you. With each flick, say:

Bad luck, be gone!

Afterwards, hold your hands over your heart, and visualize the light of the candle completely filling your entire body and aura, burning away negativity and transmuting it into positive energy and the best possible luck. Finish by smudging yourself with the incense.

Tess Whitehurst

 December 29

Monday

2nd ♈

☽ v/c 7:46 pm

Color of the day: White
Incense of the day: Lily

Breathing New Air

The year is almost over, and the days are slowly starting to get longer again. It's time to reflect on the past year, and look forward to the new year on the horizon. What are your plans? What are your goals? A new year can mean a new start on life—not just through temporary resolutions, but through real, serious plans that you prepare and work with to make them come to fruition.

As you spend time meditating, use the following chant to help open your mind to new possibilities:

Breathing new air into my life

Helps my mind to grow.

Breathing new air into my life

Strengthens my spirit and soul.

Repeat this slowly several times over. This meditation and chant will help put your mind into the right setting to get moving on achieving those new goals.

Kerri Connor

December 30

Tuesday

2nd ♈

☽ → ♉ 5:56 am

Color of the day: Scarlet
Incense of the day: Geranium

Falling Needles Family Rest Day

Every gift has been opened, every relative and friend has visited, and way too much food has been consumed. The holidays have been celebrated in every possible way. And yet, more parties and activities begin tomorrow. If the tree is starting to look a little shabby or bare, perhaps this is the year to begin a new family tradition.

Make some quiet family time today. Light red candles to honor Mars—and to build up personal power. Try to avoid electronic distractions. Pack away the ornaments and most decorations. Put gifts in their new proper places. Create a charity box for any old items that may have been replaced with new ones. Take down the tree: if fake, put it back in the box or storage space, and if live, dispose of it in the most environmentally friendly fashion. Eat lightly, drink plenty of water, take a short walk, and nap at least once. Extinguish the candles and go to bed early in preparation for the next two days of renewed celebration.

Emyme

 December 31

Wednesday

2nd ♉

Color of the day: Yellow
Incense of the day: Bay laurel

New Year's Eve

Auld Lang Syne

Use the energy of New Year's Eve to bring about a reunion with someone from the past.

Set up an altar with pink candles and a picture of your "old acquaintance." Sing the song "Auld Lang Syne" while visualizing a reunion with this person. Gaze at the candles and the picture while sending energy into a positive, happy meeting.

Go to a New Year's Eve party. From time to time at the party, allow your thoughts to include your old acquaintance.

At midnight, sing "Auld Lang Syne" again, letting the joy of the event push the energy outward into the universe, speeding its way to your friend. Naturally, the spell is sealed with a kiss!

Bring home a party favor or memento from the evening, and place it on the altar. Your reunion is on its way!

Deborah Lipp

Daily Magical Influences

Each day is ruled by a planet that possesses specific magical influences:

Monday (Moon): peace, healing, caring, psychic awareness, purification.

Tuesday (Mars): passion, sex, courage, aggression, protection.

Wednesday (Mercury): conscious mind, study, travel, divination, wisdom.

Thursday (Jupiter): expansion, money, prosperity, generosity.

Friday (Venus): love, friendship, reconciliation, beauty.

Saturday (Saturn): longevity, exorcism, endings, homes, houses.

Sunday (Sun): healing, spirituality, success, strength, protection.

Lunar Phases

The lunar phase is important in determining best times for magic.

The waxing moon (from the new moon to the full moon) is the ideal time for magic to draw things toward you.

The full moon is the time of greatest power.

The waning moon (from the full moon to the new moon) is a time for study, meditation, and little magical work (except magic designed to banish harmful energies).

Astrological Symbols

The Sun	☉	Aries	♈
The Moon	☽	Taurus	♉
Mercury	☿	Gemini	♊
Venus	♀	Cancer	♋
Mars	♂	Leo	♌
Jupiter	♃	Virgo	♍
Saturn	♄	Libra	♎
Uranus	♅	Scorpio	♏
Neptune	♆	Sagittarius	♐
Pluto	♇	Capricorn	♑
		Aquarius	♒
		Pisces	♓

The Moon's Sign

The moon's sign is a traditional consideration for astrologers. The moon continuously moves through each sign in the zodiac, from Aries to Pisces. The moon influences the sign it inhabits, creating different energies that affect our daily lives.

Aries: Good for starting things but lacks staying power. Things occur rapidly but quickly pass. People tend to be argumentative and assertive.

Taurus: Things begun now do last, tend to increase in value, and become hard to alter. Brings out an appreciation for beauty and sensory experience.

Gemini: Things begun now are easily changed by outside influence. Time for shortcuts, communications, games, and fun.

Cancer: Stimulates emotional rapport between people. Pinpoints need, supports growth and nurturance. Tend to domestic concerns.

Leo: Draws emphasis to the self, to central ideas or institutions, away from connections with others and emotional needs. People tend to be melodramatic.

Virgo: Favors accomplishment of details and commands from higher up. Focus on health, hygiene, and daily schedules.

Libra: Favors cooperation, compromise, social activities, beautification of surroundings, balance, and partnership.

Scorpio: Increases awareness of psychic power. Favors activities requiring intensity and focus. People tend to brood and become secretive under this moon sign.

Sagittarius: Encourages flights of imagination and confidence. This moon sign is adventurous, philosophical, and athletic. Favors expansion and growth.

Capricorn: Develops strong structure. Focus on traditions, responsibilities, and obligations. A good time to set boundaries and rules.

Aquarius: Rebellious energy. Time to break habits and make abrupt change. Personal freedom and individuality are the focus.

Pisces: The focus is on dreaming, nostalgia, intuition, and psychic impressions. A good time for spiritual or philanthropic activities.

Glossary of Magical Terms

Altar: A low table that holds magical tools as a focus for spell workings.

Athame: A ritual knife used to direct personal power during workings or to symbolically draw diagrams in a spell. It is rarely, if ever, used for actual physical cutting.

Aura: An invisible energy field surrounding a person. The aura can change color depending on the state of the individual.

Balefire: A fire lit for magical purposes, usually outdoors.

Casting a circle: The process of drawing a circle around oneself to seal out unfriendly influences and raise magical power. It is the first step in a spell.

Censer: An incense burner. Traditionally a censer is a metal container, filled with incense, that is swung on the end of a chain.

Censing: The process of burning incense to spiritually cleanse an object.

Centering yourself: To prepare for a magical rite by calming and centering all of your personal energy.

Chakra: One of the seven centers of spiritual energy in the human body, according to the philosophy of yoga.

Charging: To infuse an object with magical power.

Circle of protection: A circle cast to protect oneself from unfriendly influences.

Crystals: Quartz or other stones that store cleansing or protective energies.

Deosil: Clockwise movement, symbolic of life and positive energies.

Deva: A divine being according to Hindu beliefs; a devil or evil spirit according to Zoroastrianism.

Direct/retrograde: Refers to the motion of a planet when seen from the earth. A planet is "direct" when it appears to be moving forward from the point of view of a person on the earth. It is "retrograde" when it appears to be moving backward.

Dowsing: To use a divining rod to search for a thing, usually water or minerals.

Dowsing pendulum: A long cord with a coin or gem at one end. The pattern of its swing is used to predict the future.

Dryad: A tree spirit or forest guardian.

Fey: An archaic term for a magical spirit or a fairylike being.

Gris-gris: A small bag containing charms, herbs, stones, and other items to draw energy, luck, love, or prosperity to the wearer.

Mantra: A sacred chant used in Hindu tradition to embody the divinity invoked; it is said to possess deep magical power.

Needfire: A ceremonial fire kindled at dawn on major Wiccan holidays. It was traditionally used to light all other household fires.

Pentagram: A symbolically protective five-pointed star with one point upward.

Power hand: The dominant hand; the hand used most often.

Scry: To predict the future by gazing at or into an object such as a crystal ball or pool of water.

Second sight: The psychic power or ability to foresee the future.

Sigil: A personal seal or symbol.

Smudge/smudge stick: To spiritually cleanse an object by waving smoke over and around it. A smudge stick is a bundle of several incense sticks.

Wand: A stick or rod used for casting circles and as a focus for magical power.

Widdershins: Counterclockwise movement, symbolic of negative magical purposes, sometimes used to disperse negative energies.

Spell Notes

Spell Notes

Spell Notes

Llewellyn's 2014 Witches' Line!

Packed with an astounding array of content, it's no wonder *Llewellyn's Witches' Calendar* is the top-selling calendar of its kind. It includes articles, astrological data, daily correspondences, and original full-color artwork by Kathleen Edwards.

Llewellyn's Witches' Datebook is perfect for the Witch on the go. Much more than an appointment book and calendar, this multipurpose datebook allows you to blend the magical and the mundane while keeping pace with the ever-turning Wheel of the Year. Find seasonal spells, moon rituals, sabbat recipes, astrological information, and articles, all punctuated by Edwards' inspiring artwork.

GET MORE AT LLEWELLYN.COM

Visit us online to browse hundreds of our books and decks, plus sign up to receive our e-newsletters and exclusive online offers.

- **Free tarot readings • Spell-A-Day • Moon phases**
- **Recipes, spells, and tips • Blogs • Encyclopedia**
- **Author interviews, articles, and upcoming events**

GET SOCIAL WITH LLEWELLYN

Find us on **Facebook**

www.Facebook.com/LlewellynBooks

Follow us on

www.Twitter.com/Llewellynbooks

GET BOOKS AT LLEWELLYN

LLEWELLYN ORDERING INFORMATION

Order online: Visit our website at www.llewellyn.com to select your books and place an order on our secure server.

Order by phone:
- Call toll free within the U.S. at 1-877-NEW-WRLD (1-877-639-9753)
- Call toll free within Canada at 1-866-NEW-WRLD (1-866-639-9753)
- We accept VISA, MasterCard, and American Express

Order by mail:
Send the full price of your order (MN residents add 6.875% sales tax) in U.S. funds, plus postage and handling to: Llewellyn Worldwide, 2143 Wooddale Drive Woodbury, MN 55125-2989

POSTAGE AND HANDLING
STANDARD (U.S. & Canada):
(Please allow 12 business days)
$25.00 and under, add $4.00.
$25.01 and over, FREE SHIPPING.

INTERNATIONAL ORDERS (airmail only):
$16.00 for one book, plus $3.00 for each additional book.

Visit us online for more shipping options. Prices subject to change.

FREE CATALOG!

To order, call
1-877-NEW-WRLD
ext. 8236
or visit our
website